Twayne's English Authors Series

EDITOR OF THIS VOLUME

Kinley E. Roby

Northeastern University

J. R. R. Tolkien

TEAS 304

J. R. R. TOLKIEN

By DEBORAH WEBSTER ROGERS
and IVOR A. ROGERS

TWAYNE PUBLISHERS

A DIVISION OF G. K. HALL & CO., BOSTON

Printed on permanent/durable acid-free paper and bound
in the United States of America

Photograph of J.R.R. Tolkien by Charles Huttar

Library of Congress Cataloging in Publication Data

Rogers, Deborah Webster and Rogers, Ivor A.
J. R. R. Tolkien.

(Twayne's English authors series; TEAS 304)
Bibliography: p. 151
Includes index.
1.   Tolkien, John Ronald Reuel, 1892–1973—
Criticism and interpretation.
PR6039.032Z816   828'.91209   80-11518
ISBN 0-8057-6796-7

To the
University of Wisconsin
J. R. R. Tolkien Society
1966–

Contents

About the Authors

Deborah Rogers has been a Tolkienist since third grade, when she was given *The Hobbit* (original version). She read *The Lord of the Rings* as it came out, and in her last year at Milton Academy gave a talk on Tolkien. In preparing for it, she wrote him a letter to which his answer forms the appendix of this book (what is a Tolkien book without an appendix?). She majored in French and German at Saint Michael's College in the University of Toronto, taking her junior year abroad. Going into comparative literature, she wrote her master's essay at Columbia on the theatrical fantasist Jean Giraudoux, the same year Richard Plotz founded the Tolkien Society of America. At the University of Wisconsin, Professor Fannie LeMoine encouraged Professor Rogers to write her doctoral dissertation on Tolkien and C. S. Lewis.

Ivor A. Rogers, a former professor of theater, collaborates with his wife on scholarly works. He was a founder of the Science Fiction Research Association and the University of Wisconsin Tolkien Society.

Preface

In a hole in the ground there lived a hobbit. Not a nasty,
dirty, wet hole, filled with the ends of worms and an oozy
smell, nor yet a dry, bare, sandy hole with nothing in it
to sit down on or to eat: it was a hobbit-hole, and that
means comfort.[1]

J. R. R. Tolkien, *The Hobbit*

In a scholar's mind there lived an artist. Not a nasty, dirty,
prying mind, filled with other people's private affairs and an
oozy smell; nor yet a dry, bare, factual mind with nothing in
it to marvel or laugh at: it was Professor Tolkien's mind, and
that means magic. Though he lived an apparently circumscribed
life as an Oxford don, the publication of his fiction revealed that
his imagination could circumscribe ("write round") the whole
globe; and readers round the globe have immersed themselves
in his tales of hobbits and the history of Middle-earth.

He did not, single-handedly, transform public taste and publishing practice;[2] but his work is so outstanding and his influence so conspicuous that his name stands first: Tolkien and
twentieth-century fantasy, like Shakespeare and Elizabethan
drama.[3] From the time his tales came out in paperbacks (1965),
bookracks everywhere display not only those books, but their
influence: in other stories, cover artwork, blurbs, and even styles
of lettering.

Successful books are followed by books and articles about
them. Some years ago, I was asked to speak on "What's Wrong
with Tolkien Criticism?" The first answer was, "In itself, nothing." The field of Tolkien studies is in even better shape now,
with the works of Carpenter, Foster, Kocher, and West. The
only thing wrong with Tolkien criticism—any criticism—would be
to consider it more important than the works which inspired it.
To imply to any reader that any critical work—even the best—
were the one gate to the sheepfold would be wrong entirely.

The text, Tolkien's own work, is the important thing. Readers settling down with a secondary work should consider whether their time might be better spent rereading the text.

There remains the consideration that Tolkien himself was not happy about "Tolkien criticism." Much of the criticism practiced in his times was by disciples of Freud (or if not true disciples, at least such as said to Freud, "Lord! Lord!"). Their tenet that everything was really about sex was applied to art and artists alike. There is also plain muckraking. "Modern 'researchers' inform me that Beethoven cheated his publishers, and abominably ill-treated his nephew; but I do not believe that has anything to do with his music," wrote Tolkien.[4] Both Freudianism and muckraking applied wholesale become obnoxious.[5]

But for Tolkien to discourage all criticism would be first impossible and second illogical. Impossible because lovers of his stories, like other enthusiasts, *will* act. They may try to get in touch with Tolkien himself; in fact, he became quite burdened by rude fans. They may congregate, talk, dress up, feast; and they may write stories, poems, and criticism ranging from "The Geology of Middle-earth" to "Tolkien's Fairy-tale Morality."[6]

As for the logic of criticism, it follows the logic of Tolkien's own argument about art in "On Fairy Stories."[7] He stated that the human artist is a subcreator, building "a Secondary World which your mind can enter." "We make still by the law in which we're made," he continued (*TR*, 54). That is, mankind is the Creator's work of art, and has in itself something of His love of making beautiful things, which man then exercises as best he can. Now, for human beings to be so moved by primary creation that they seek its Artist is obviously good. Human study will never encompass God, but to pursue the study in any way shows a laudable spirit in the creature. And some such effort is also fitting toward the human artist by those who love his work. As Tolkien argues with C. S. Lewis in the verse just quoted, I would argue with him for criticism:

> Worship, however clumsy, is the due
> Of the Creator—and His sublings. You
> In your degree are subject to it too.[8]

To study about Tolkien is good, to read his works better; to think the works can be explained by studying about him is a mistake. Not he nor even his guardian angel can trace the connection, he said (letter, appendix). We have no way of making the person of a genius and his works coincide in our mind.[9]

This study does not pretend to exhaustive criticism of any of Tolkien's works or days. I have ventured to describe some of his mental processes, when they can be clearly imagined from Carpenter's biography or from Tolkien's known beliefs and interests. The purpose of this book is to introduce briefly and clearly Tolkien's life (chapter 1), some of his mental furniture of a literary kind (chapter 2), and his major short works and his long fiction (chapters 3–6). The concluding chapter shows how Tolkien's art and values jointly contradict those most conspicuous in the Europe of his adulthood. The Selected Bibliography is to help Tolkienists continue their study in whatever direction they want.

DEBORAH WEBSTER ROGERS

Des Moines

Acknowledgments

Special thanks to the Estate of J. R. R. Tolkien for permission to publish his letter, the Appendix of this study. The Houghton Mifflin Company has allowed quotations from the American editions of Tolkien's works and Humphrey Carpenter's *Tolkien*. Portions of this text have appeared in other forms.

Many friends have furthered my Tolkien studies. Of particular help with this book, for anecdotal material, scriptural knowledge, help with the index, etc., have been Bill Connet, Patty Donham, jan finder, Alan Jensen, Steve Kagel, Moishe Kazowitz, Steve Pokorny, Gordon Redding, Margaret Robinson and her students, Bill Smith, Jeanette Webb, and John Rateliff.

Richard West has been generous with his learning and with encouragement.

Deborah Jones Webster has provided moral support and information (including spelling corrections).

A Tolkienist will not use the word precious; but the editorial help of Professor Kinley Roby has been—most valuable.

Thank you all.

Chronology

1892 January 3, John Ronald Reuel Tolkien born in Bloemfontein, South Africa, to Arthur and Mabel Suffield Tolkien.

1895 Returns to England.

1896 Father dies in South Africa.

1904 Mother dies.

1908 Meets Edith Bratt.

1911 Enters Exeter College, Oxford University.

1916 Marries Edith. To war in France; invalided home.

1917 Begins writing his mythology. Son John born.

1918 War ends; "all but one of my close friends were dead."

1920 Teaching post at Leeds University. Son Michael born.

1924 Son Christopher born.

1925 Tolkien and Gordon edition of *Sir Gawain and the Green Knight* published. Professorship at Oxford.

1929 Daughter Priscilla born.

1936 Lecture on *Beowulf: the Monsters and the Critics.*

1937 *The Hobbit.*

1939 Lecture "On Fairy Stories."

1949 *Farmer Giles of Ham.*

1954– *The Lord of the Rings.*

1955

1959 Retires from Oxford.

1962 *The Adventures of Tom Bombadil.*

1964 *Tree and Leaf.*

1965 Early in the year, unauthorized American paperback publication of *The Lord of the Rings;* autumn, authorized paperback; start of "Tolkien boom."

1967 *Smith of Wootton Major.*

1968 Ronald and Edith Tolkien move to Bournemouth.

1971 Edith dies.

1972 Tolkien returns to Oxford.

1973 September 2, Tolkien dies.

1975 Translations of *Sir Gawain, Pearl,* and *Sir Orfeo.*

1977 *The Silmarillion,* edited by son Christopher.

CHAPTER 1

A Modest Life

TOLKIEN'S stories are gorgeous: not his circumstances. For his chosen life, he could have written his own version of Horace's ode:

> My boy, I loathe these Persian flummeries
> And orchids flown from where late summer is.
> Weave garlands from the land where you were born,
> And deck us both with oak and ash and thorn.

Arthur Tolkien, a bank manager, and his wife Mabel Suffield Tolkien had their first baby in South Africa in 1892. John Ronald Reuel was rosy, with true blue eyes and a fuzz of fair hair on his high-domed head. One of the family's servants was so fascinated that he took him home without asking, to show his fellow-villagers, who had never met a white baby. Despite the family's alarm, they understood what had happened and continued to employ the servant, who in gratitude gave his own son "Mister Tolkien" as a middle name.

It is easy to imagine that the young Tolkien—in South Africa and the Orange Free State at that—may have seen and been enchanted with the splendor of diamonds. His *Hobbit* and *Silmarillion* suggest as much. We can be fairly certain that the baby was held by a parent, as they looked at the constellations of the southern hemisphere, and sung to:

> Twinkle, twinkle, little star!
> How I wonder what you are,
> Up above the world so high,
> Like a diamond in the sky.

What his mind did with this bit of lore will be seen in chapter 5.

Ronald Tolkien did not stay long in the country of Zulus, sun, and tarantulas. Because he never throve in the climate of the Orange Free State, his mother took him to England when he was three and his brother Hilary one. They intended a visit to her parents, the Suffields, in Birmingham.

Unfortunately, his father died after rheumatic fever within a year. The three repatriated Tolkiens never returned to South Africa, and the boy's memories grew dim—with sudden jars like expecting the Bloemfontein verandah on the Birmingham house.

With little money, Mabel Tolkien and the boys found a house and eked out an existence in the green and quiet village of Sarehole (now unrecognizably engulfed by the city of Birmingham). In 1896, the Tolkiens found themselves among plump, provincial-minded country people, some kind, some cross; and among mushrooms, berries, and trees, about which Mrs. Tolkien knew quite a lot and passed it on to her sons. Hilary grew up to be a fruit farmer.

She also tutored them in other subjects she knew, notably Latin and French, drawing, and music. Ronald lapped up Latin, did not care for French, and liked to draw: a pleasure which never left him. He also read stories, including that of Sigurd and Fafnir. Inspired to try his own hand, the boy produced a small tale involving a "green great dragon."

Didn't he mean a great green dragon, asked his mother.

"Why?"

Mabel Tolkien did not know, though she was positive about the correct usage. John Ronald Reuel continued asking Why about language for seventy more years.

In 1900 Mabel Tolkien became a Roman Catholic: a matter of scandal and woe to her Unitarian, Baptist, and Anglican relatives and in-laws. The ecumenical spirit of the 1960s was still far off. The Vatican had condemned Anglican Holy Orders as invalid four years earlier; and the Church of England had been divesting itself of ritual after ritual, seeing them as "Popish." The Anglican church held that the Roman Catholic church had seceded from true Catholicism in the sixteenth century, and the dissenting sects also found little to love in the Roman church.

Tolkien retained the impression that the coolness in the family had hastened his mother's death; she died of diabetes at thirty-four, when Ronald was twelve and Hilary ten. The boy who could say, like Goethe, that he had inherited "From dear Mama my cheerfulness / And love of storytelling" now bore the pain of her death.

At least the two orphans were not all alone, for she had left as their guardian the vivid and affectionate priest, her friend Father Francis Xavier Morgan. He belonged to the Oratory, an English congregation on whose grounds the Tolkien family had spent their lovely last summer together.[1] Father Francis used some money he had from his family to help the boys, and he gave Ronald the run of his Spanish books. His wards went to room with an aunt, lately widowed, who did not repudiate "Romans." But her household was not nurturing and happy for boys, so three years later Father Francis found them a room in a Mrs. Faulkner's house.

There they met and became allies with the pretty, grey-eyed Edith Bratt, with whom they used to smuggle midnight snacks. She too was an orphan, with training in piano playing, but frustrated by Mrs. Faulkner in her practicing. Ronald and Edith fell in love and wanted to marry. Father Francis, hearing of their attachment by rumor, took it very ill. Edith was only twenty and not a Catholic; Tolkien was only seventeen, and in his next-to-last year at school. The guardian forbade their marriage and did all he could to keep them apart. But when at last Tolkien came of age and did marry Edith, Father Francis acquiesced gracefully.

Tolkien finished school at King Edward's with a record distinguished, though not earth-shattering. As well as advancing in Latin and learning Greek, like all the boys, he had discovered Middle English and Anglo-Saxon (Old English), with help from George Brewerton, an English-master with medieval interests.

On his second try, Tolkien won an exhibition (a small scholarship) to Exeter College, Oxford, to which he "went up" in the autumn of 1911. His interests were not all academic. Not that he and his comrades *often* hijacked city busses; but what with eating, drinking, and always talking, Tolkien's academic record and his purse were pretty thin. He was supposed to be reading (majoring in) classics.

World War I overtook that generation. Tolkien joined a

program which combined officers' training with finishing his B.A.,
and became a second lieutenant trained in signaling in the
Lancashire Fusiliers. Before being posted to France in the
spring of 1916, he was finally able to marry his Edith, who then
led a peripatetic life for the rest of the war, in the company of
her older cousin Jennie. They gave each other moral support and
got on each other's nerves.

Lieutenant Tolkien, his luggage lost, was sent to the Somme
amid every sort of discomfort and danger, and stationed at the
village of Bouzincourt. The battlefield was not like signaling
school. It was not even the way the commanding officers thought
it was; they would send heavily laden Tommies marching into
barbed wire which they assured them had been cut. Gas was in
use, damaging both the side trying to use it and the side meant
to receive it. What consolation Tolkien could find came from
glimpses of his school friend Geoffrey Smith, in another battalion
of the same regiment; and from seeing the unpretentious perseverance—sometimes humor-leavened, sometimes grim—of the
lower ranks. It was borne in on him that the great sum, heroism,
was made up of little, matter-of-fact doing-my-duties.[2]

That autumn he came down with trench fever, carried to
everyone by lice, and was shipped home. Part of his convales-
cence was spent on the Holderness peninsula in the northeast of
England, where Edith, now the mother of tiny John, sang and
danced in a glade of hemlock flowers, which resemble Queen
Anne's lace. Tolkien's feelings of having been lost and then finding the loveliest thing on Earth crystallized round this image,
as he allowed his readers to see years later in (Aragorn's song of
Beren and Luthien:)

> The leaves were long, the grass was green,
>   The hemlock-umbels tall and fair,
> And in the glade a light was seen
>   Of stars in shadow shimmering.
> Tinúviel was dancing there
>   To music of a pipe unseen,
> And light of stars was in her hair,
>   And in her raiment glimmering.
>
> There Beren came from mountains cold

> And lost he wandered under leaves,
> And where the Elven-river rolled
> He walked alone and sorrowing.
> He peered between the hemlock-leaves
> And saw in wonder flowers of gold
> Upon her mantle and her sleeves,
> And her hair like shadow following.[3]

The story of these lovers was part of a cycle of tales in verse and prose which Tolkien had been working on since his teens. Now, recovering from his fever, he read them to Edith, who wrote them fair in a notebook for him: "The Book of Lost Tales."

His body kept him laid up with recurrences of fever in this or that infirmary for the rest of the war.

The war's physical cruelty to Tolkien had been minor; not so its psychological cruelty: "By 1918 all but one of my close friends were dead" (I, xi). As Smith had written just before his own death, "Oh my dear John Ronald what ever are we going to do?"[4] First his parents, now his comrades. Tolkien's sense of the passing of good times and wonderful people, never to be recovered in this world, shows clearly in his stories to the end of his life.

In November, 1918, the war ended, and the three Tolkiens and Jennie Grove settled in Oxford, where Ronald had a job working on the New English Dictionary. The hiring of such a young man by the senior philologists was a tribute to his expertise in the field, for the dictionary is one of the world's monuments of thoroughness. Years later, a publisher objected to Tolkien's spelling "dwarves," pointing out that the *OED* gives the plural "dwarfs." Tolkien, superbly: "I *wrote* the *Oxford English Dictionary!*"[5]

In Oxford, dons' (teachers') wives for decades have been treated as a lowly order, and Mrs. Tolkien was not the lady to fight for more. She was happier at Leeds, in the North, where Tolkien was invited to a teaching post in the English department. Again, as during the war, he was impressed and pleased with the patient, hard work of the ordinary stodgy students. Tolkien as a teacher was unpredictable: he could recreate a medieval banquet round his students, he could chant like a bard, he *could* explain clearly and trenchantly; he could also wander off into byways of thought, and mumble.[6] To Leeds came E. V. Gordon, a Canadian, whom Tolkien found a most congenial colleague. Together they edited *Sir Gawain and the Green Knight*, a Middle English romance; their edition, revised, is still in use.

The Tolkiens went back to Oxford in 1925, now with eight-year-old John, five-year-old Michael, and new Christopher. There ensued the family's longest period without external movement: they lived in or near Oxford until 1968.

Tolkien was the Rawlinson and Bosworth Professor of Anglo-Saxon; each subject had only one teacher with the title of professor. As the department had hoped when they hired him, he undertook with gusto the healing of ill-will in the English School (department). There was jealousy between the "language side" and the "literature side": between those studying Anglo-Saxon, Middle English, and literature to 1400 and those studying English literature after 1400. "Never trust a philologist," newcomers on the Literature side were warned.[7] Politicking was fun for Tolkien, and of course he was devoted to his field; but being a man of good-will and sense, and an articulate speaker (though not eloquent: his delivery was often hard to follow, rapid, and soft), he helped in revising the School's curriculum and quieting intradepartmental jealousies.[8]

He also made friends, after the pitiful sweep of the Kaiser's war. Notable among them was Jack (C. S.) Lewis, a zestful bachelor who liked his friends to gather in his rooms in Magdalen College (pronounced maudlin), to read aloud whatever they were writing and to talk, discuss, and argue about whatever might arise. Lewis wrote poems and was working on a book about courtly love (see chapter 2, section II); his brother Warnie might bring an essay on France under the Sun-King, Louis XIV;[9] sharing this seventeenth-century interest was Hugo Dyson, a man even more cat-quick than the rest with a pun or an argument. To each other, these men were not Olympian scholars, but friends; among them was no kid-glove respect. If they did not like, understand, or believe what someone wrote, they *said* so, as tellingly as they could, in all good-will.

Their friend Tollers, Ronald Tolkien, would sometimes read comical rhymes and sometimes stories which sounded like old lore, and in the 1930s had written down a good deal of a children's book, "The Hobbit." The Inklings, this loose group round Lewis, enjoyed the story, but it did not seem important enough to Tolkien to finish. At last, by neat footwork, two Oxford English graduates (Elaine Griffiths and Susan Dagnall) now working for a publisher, achieved both the manuscript and its completion. The publisher's ten-year-old son, Rayner Unwin, concurring, *The Hobbit* was published by Allen and Unwin in 1937, with pictures by the author; and the field of children's literature had a new ornament.

Dyson, who preferred conversation to reading, in later years kept the group as a whole from hearing a good deal of Tolkien's stories.[10]

When World War II, threatening London, drove the Oxford University Press back to its parent university, Charles Williams arrived. He was older than Lewis and Tolkien, and already a noted writer of fiction in which the everyday world crosses the plane of the supernatural; "spiritual thrillers," his novels have been called. T. S. Eliot observes that to Williams, "the supernatural was perfectly natural, and the natural was also supernatural."[11] Williams, Lewis, and Tolkien saw each other regularly. Lewis, with assistance from Doctor Havard, was studying the problem of pain. Tolkien was reading from "the new Hobbit," or "The Lord of the Rings," as it came to be called. Williams wrote religious drama and Arthurian lyrics and planned a book-length study, "The Figure of Arthur." In the spring when Hitler's Germany was defeated, Williams died. Lewis mourned especially. "Now that Charles is dead, I shall never again see Ronald's reaction to a specifically Caroline joke. Far from having more of Ronald, having him 'to myself' now that Charles is away, I have less of Ronald."[12]

Tolkien, though he had enjoyed Williams's company, had not admired nor been friends with him so deeply as Lewis had. The men's stories sometimes seem to murmur with each other's crosscurrents, but on the question of Influence, Lewis wrote, "No one ever influenced Tolkien—you might as well try to influence a bandersnatch. We listened to his work, but could affect it only by encouragement. He has only two reactions to criticism; either he begins the whole work over again from the beginning

or else he takes no notice at all."[13] The "bandersnatch" replied
that he had indeed ignored Lewis's *suggestions*; "but when he
said, 'You can do better. Better, Tolkien, please,' I used to try."[14]

Tolkien's scholarly work had never appeared at a blazing pace.
After *The Hobbit* and after World War II, he was supposed to
be editing the *Ancrene Wisse*, a booklet of advice for anchoresses,
ladies living holy and secluded lives outside convents. It is in
Middle English, some of the manuscripts in Tolkien's beloved
West Midland dialect. His edition did not appear and did not
appear, to the impatience of scholars in the field. Also not appearing was a projected Tolkien and Gordon edition of *The Pearl*,
a companion volume to *Sir Gawain and the Green Knight*, which
is probably by the same poet. Gordon died unexpectedly in 1938:
another friend to be missed. Tolkien put *The Pearl* in and out
of his *Who's Who* entries for years, until Ida Gordon, Eric's
widow, picked up the project and finished it herself.

Tolkien's work on *Gawain* and *The Pearl* finally resulted in
translations of them. His modern English *Gawain* was broadcast
by the BBC in 1953, with introductory words he had written.
These translations and that of another Middle English romance,
"Sir Orfeo," were published by Christopher Tolkien after his
father's death.

Allen and Unwin were finding that Tolkien's juveniles—now
they wanted more—were not appearing at a blazing pace either.
"Mr. Bliss," which he had written and illustrated in color for his
children after his own motoring misadventures, was too difficult
to reproduce, especially with wartime shortages of printing
materials. Other tales were incomplete, and none of them dealt
with hobbits, for whom the public had conceived an affection.

As far as scholars and hobbitophiles could see, almost nothing
happened for seventeen years. The Tolkien family moved several
times, winding up in the Oxford suburb of Headington, in a
smaller house which tried Edith's arthritis less, now that the four
children were living on their own. Professor Tolkien continued
his university duties; in 1945 he was elected Merton Professor
of English Language and Literature. But anchoress-watchers and
Unwins alike could be heard muttering, "What is Tolkien doing?"

The scholars had a long wait, and some died in the meanwhile.
In 1955, Tolkien's student Mary Salu published a translation (not

an edition) of the *Ancrene Riwle*, the London-dialect version of the booklet, with a short introduction by the professor. His edition of the *Wisse* finally appeared in 1962. Editions of other manuscripts by his students are said to embody many of Tolkien's ideas.

His children and some of the Inklings, Tolkien's most faithful audiences, knew what he was doing. They had been hearing, or receiving at wartime posts, chapters from "the new Hobbit," and they had been drawn into the tale, and encouraged Tolkien to keep on. But this he could only sometimes do. What with daily life (including wartime), barren spells, his niggling thoroughness, and the constant unfolding of more in his story than he had ever suspected was there, it was not until 1950 that he could even imagine it finished.

Then he got into a lengthy go-round with two publishers: Allen and Unwin, *The Hobbit's* publisher, and Collins; because Tolkien had hopes that Collins would publish *The Lord of the Rings* along with *The Silmarillion*, Tolkien's "Book of Lost Tales," which he considered at least as important. Eventually, Collins would not print both uncut, so *The Lord of the Rings* went to Allen and Unwin. Not that the publisher was expecting to gain, except in prestige; but as Sir Stanley Unwin cabled from abroad to the now-adult Rayner, "If you think it a work of genius, you may lose £1000."[15] The six-book work was so long they decided to print it in three volumes, which at last reached the public in 1954 and 1955.

A three-volume fairy tale: *that* was what the Rawlinson and Bosworth Professor of Anglo-Saxon had been doing for seventeen years. Some of academe was frankly nettled. True, light literature is nothing new for Oxford dons: Dodgson, of Maths, called himself Lewis Carroll and wrote the *Alice* stories; Stewart, of English, calls himself Michael Innes and writes detective stories; Coghill, also of English, has based a rousing musical on Chaucer's *Canterbury Tales*. But in the 1950s, any story leading outside the three dimensions of our world got little respect from most of the literary establishment. In the United States, a publisher was writing to an author about the same time that "There is no market for fantasy."

The articulate Jack Lewis, now a widely read writer of Christian apologetics, science fiction, and juveniles, weighed in as eloquently as he could in favor of *The Lord of the Rings*. Indeed, he had been supporting Tolkien all along, though not uncritically. Other reviewers praised, panned, and misread the books. Allen and Unwin did not lose the thousand pounds; they kept having to reprint. In 1957, the daughters of J. I. M. Stewart (Michael Innes) and the daughter of an American scholar, making each other's acquaintance in Oxford, found a bond in their love of Tolkien's stories. The books seemed to work like the *Patna* incident in *Lord Jim*: if two people who knew them met, anywhere, a point would come in the conversation where they would look at each other and chorus, "Have *you* read . . . ?"

Ten years after the hardback, Tolkien's American readers were delighted to see *The Lord of Rings* coming out in paper. Then they learned that Tolkien had never given permission for that edition and was receiving no royalties from it. Another go-round with publishers was upon him. He tightened up some loose ends in the story, something he cared very much about doing anyway, and an authorized, revised paperback edition was rushed into print by Ballantine. Ace, who had printed the first one, explained that under existing copyright laws they had done no wrong, and from underneath a stack of indignant mail they reached out a substantial royalty check to Tolkien.

The "Tolkien phenomenon" took off like one of his beloved fireworks. Americans are known for enthusiasms; and here was a work of substance, beauty, variety, and endless ramification; a work, moreover, the like of which had not been promoted by publisher nor professor for decades (see chapter 2, section IV). Refreshed, exalted, energetic, waves of readers threw themselves onto the bookstands.

The Tolkiens continued living in Headington; the professor had retired in 1959. But effects from the books and their popularity were making themselves felt. Money was nice to have, after a life of having to watch pennies; not nice was being awoken by telephone calls from fans mistaken about time zones. Allen and Unwin dispatched to Tolkien's aid a special assistant for mail, Joy Hill. Some of the letters were of such sticky fulsomness that it is a wonder if she did not find ants feeding on them.

The disadvantages of being a monument, and Edith's declining health, decided the Tolkiens to move to the south coast of England, near Bournemouth where they had spent several summers. Tolkien did not find the place very congenial, but at least people did not snap pictures through the windows. After they had lived there for three years, Edith died.

Tolkien, shorn again, moved back to Oxford. Merton College had a set of rooms where they invited their honorary Fellow to live. A kind couple, the Carrs, college scouts (servants), lived downstairs and helped take care of him. Other honors from universities came to him, and from the British crown: he was given the order C.B.E., Commander of the Order of the British Empire.

With friends, with descendants, with manuscripts, crossword puzzles and loneliness, Tolkien lived in Oxford for almost two years. His digestion troubled him, then cleared up. But on a visit to Bournemouth in August, 1973, he was taken ill, and died on the second of September. His body and Edith's are buried in Wolvercote cemetery near Oxford. On their stones are engraved the names BEREN and LUTHIEN.

The "Tolkien phenomenon" has not ceased with his death. As he and Christopher had agreed, Christopher bravely undertook the editing of *The Silmarillion*, for which publishers and public had again been waiting. Four years later he had it done, having dealt with papers from typescripts through the "Lost Tales" notebook to the backs of envelopes. It was published in 1977: another ringing success, though *The Silmarillion* differs again from *The Hobbit* and *The Lord of the Rings* as much as they do from each other.

Clearly, Tolkien's unpretentious life was like the wardrobe in C. S. Lewis's *Lion, the Witch and the Wardrobe*, larger inside than outside.[16]

CHAPTER 2

Literary Backgrounds

THE forepart of the wardrobe was stocked with good old fur coats. Tolkien's imagination was stocked with the stories of many cultures. Sections headed "Myth," "Medieval," and "Morris" will deal briefly with three literary streams which nourished his interests—not that their channels can be sharply divided; the "Modern" section will look at the literature of Tolkien's own time, against which his work stood out so sharply. To each stream, it turns out, Tolkien has contributed: his fans would say, with W. S. Gilbert, "From Ovid and Horace to Swinburne and Morris / They all of them take a back place."

I Myth

"Mythos" in Greek means story; myths are stories which explain. Mythical explanation, unlike scientific explanation, involves value judgments: one star may be brighter than the rest, mythologically, because the hero it commemorates was dear to the gods; scientifically, because of the relation between its magnitude and its position relative to the earth.

Since human beings have the faculties to seek explanations, make value judgments, and tell stories, every human culture has its mythology. All these story cycles relate the individual to God, to the cosmos, to other people, and to himself.[1] People may not know consciously or be able to recite smoothly what myths they are living by; an individual may even be living by inconsistent mythologies.

Mythologies are first passed on by word of mouth. After centuries, when a culture has acquired writing, its mythology can be gathered into documents; the compilers may be more or less strenuous in their efforts to straighten out inconsistencies.

28

The Bible of Judaism and Christianity is the principal mythic documentary collection for Tolkien's part of space-time.

Myths tell of many things: the cosmos; the world, its elements, its creatures; mankind; gods; beginning; ending. All around the globe, mythologies bear striking resemblances, as well as their intriguing differences. It occurs to scholars that this may be because all peoples from Polynesia to Thule may be talking about the same thing.

In listening to the myths of the world, one learns that the myth-hero is found in a cave. The sound of many waters is audible in the gloom. He has left his village and is on his way to slay the resident monster. He will return with its treasure to his kindred, possibly accompanied by his bride.

Myth-scholars have concluded at various times that the hero *is* a planted grain; the sun at night; the moon at its darkness; a person in the recesses of his mind. These single interpretations have power. We all depend on the sun, which seems to go away and return. Many cultures have depended on a grain which goes down into the dark earth; lies hidden, imperiled by hungry creatures; and rises out of a split husk as a fresh shoot, bearing an ear of many full grains. And many persons have entered a frightening unknown region mentally, dealt with distressing memories or decisions, and rejoined their neighbors with fresh strength to share. Some cultures formalize the venture into adult life with initiation rituals; some offer the journey of psychoanalysis. The time may recur in the mythic eternal cycle when scholars think that myths are about many things; or perhaps that the single theme of all mythologies is a transcendent matter, expressible to our race only under the figures of sun, grain, cave, or mind.

Tolkien's Western European culture derives mostly from two others, each with its mythology: the Graeco-Roman or classical, and the Judeo-Christian. A Jew or Christian need not take umbrage at the phrase "Judeo-Christian myth"; a mythology is a body of stories allowing for value judgments, and indeed our heritage of Scripture and tradition has such. The word myth does not indicate the stories' truth or falsehood.[2]

As Christianity grew within Roman culture, the mingled classical and Hebraic streams flowed north and west into the terri-

tory of a third mythology, the Germanic or Norse. This body of
tales and lore was circulating unsystematically, orally; important
parts of it got written down in Iceland in the thirteenth century after Christ. Two key documents for Norse mythology are
the *Elder (Poetic) Edda* and the *Younger (Prose) Edda*. The
Elder is a collection of poems, whose material must go back
before 1000 A.D. but was probably collected in writing not far
from 1200 A.D. Few of the poems are narrative: most expand on
one point in a story, assuming the reader knows the story. But
the *Prose Edda*, a three-part work, in its first section presents
its mythological material in a relatively systematic way. The
author, Snorri Sturluson, is composing a guide for younger poets,
lest they forget Iceland's old lore and old, polished style of
poetry.

In Iceland, the simultaneous arrival of Christianity and
writing contributed to the preservation of the mythology even
while attacking its beliefs. In cultures without writing, a mythology could gradually be wiped out of a people's memory when
it was no longer held as the explanation of the world. Bits would
survive in folktales, but such coherence as there had been would
be lost.

A lover of folktales could then, like an archaeologist, try to
reconstruct the mythology. This was done by the bright-eyed
nineteenth-century doctor Elias Lönnrot for his native Finland.
He collected and produced *The Kalevala* (1849, final edition):
a monument of his hard work, a notably successful gathering of
myth-lore, and a book which impressed Tolkien in his teens.
Lönnrot in Finland, the Grimms collecting nursery tales and
mythology in Germany, and Longfellow composing *Hiawatha*
from American Indian stories (in Lönnrot's meter) exemplify
the nineteenth century's interest in mythology, of which section
III says more.

Tolkien, having learned classical mythology and been moved
by Norse, and finding the Finnish gathered by a modern lover
of tales, wished "that we had more of it left—something of the
same sort that belonged to the English." It came into his mind
"to make a body of more or less connected legend, ranging from
the large and cosmogonic to the level of the romantic fairy-
story . . . which I could dedicate simply: to England; to my

country." He wanted it "redolent of our 'air' (the clime and soil of the North West . . .). The cycles should be linked to a majestic whole, and yet leave scope for other minds and hands, wielding paint and music and drama. Absurd," wrote Tolkien later, and did it.[3] As Lewis might have toasted him, "Here's to J.R.R.T., may his shade not diminish, / In mythology versed from Astarte to Finnish."

He had company in missing a mythology for England. The seventeenth-century poet John Milton had decided the land needed an epic, and set out to write the "Arthuriad," from the tales of the legend-crowned king. But he found the material cramped his style, so instead wrote *Paradise Lost* and *Paradise Regained*, about the fall of man and Jesus's life. Something similar overtook Tolkien, but not so completely: after years of pondering his mythic history of archangelic powers and global upheavals, he focused his maturest work on hobbits.

Tolkien, like Milton, saw that the rich Arthurian material, much as he enjoyed it, would not do for a mythology. For the Arthur cycle as we have it is explicitly Christian: set in Christian times, and usually told by Christian writers to Christian audiences. Christian times cannot serve as the setting for a mythology comparable to the classical or Norse; the relation between man and God, and therefore between man and the rest of creation, has been changed too drastically.

Mythology sets the little in relation to the large: shows the human individual small beside the cosmos, demiurgic powers, and the Creator. But according to Christian belief, God has done the opposite: put the large in relation to the little. The Creator, bypassing all things else, made Himself a human individual.[4] This demands a shift in the human race's attention: our proper study really *is* man, and not such a trivial subject as we sometimes feel. As the girl in the folksong says, "If the King's Son loves me, I'm not so ugly as the soldiers said."[5] Our race has been given transcendent importance.

In joining this race of creatures, the supreme Being of eternity involved itself in this world's time: in history. Historic time gains an importance in stories of the Christian era which it lacks in mythologies. "When Herod was tetrarch of Galilee and Philip his brother tetrarch of Iturea and Trachonitis" sets an account

quite differently from "When the beasts could talk" or Tolkien's
"When the moon was new and the sun young."[6]

Though Christianity still involves myths, symbols, and non-
human beings, now history, literal objects, and human persons
matter more. So a writer composing a mythic account would
have trouble setting it in the Christian age because first, it would
collide with known history and second, it would reflect relations among mankind, God, and the rest of creation which have
been superseded by Jesus's life. Milton and Tolkien seem both
to have perceived that, and quit the Christian court of Arthur
for epochs long past. Chapter 5 discusses the upshot of Tolkien's
mythopoeic urge.

II *Medieval*

The term "middle ages" is used for the period from about
500 to 1500. Europe then saw itself as the heir of classical culture, as Chrétien de Troyes said in the twelfth century:

> Knighthood, we read, in Greece was praised;
> There first the lamp of Learning blazed.
> Knighthood and Learning moved to Rome,
> And now in France they make their home;
> God keep them here in years to come.

What was going on in the languages of Europe during this
time, and its works of art made with language, interested Tolkien.

Latin, spread from horizon to horizon by the Roman Empire,
was the international and the serious language. You could talk
it with Father Hauskuld on White Ness in Iceland and Brother
Colum in his scriptorium in Ireland. You could talk it in an
English marsh with the Abbess Ethelfrith; or at the Frankish
emperor's court in Aachen; or fluently in the Swiss Alps with
Brother Notker of St. Gallen. You could even talk it in Rome,
though the Romans' accent was funny and their grammar im-
pure; they did not realize their language had changed from
that of the Caesars. If you did not know Greek, you could talk
Latin at the Eastern emperor's court in Byzantium.

But increasingly, people bothered to write down compositions in the vernacular, the everyday language of a place. Some of the writing was recopied and some has lasted to our time. The invention of movable type in the 1430s and the establishment of England's first publishing house by Caxton in 1485 encouraged literacy and multiplied the dissemination and preservation of literature.

Brother Notker would have some trouble understanding an Icelandic skald, though assuming Brother Notker spoke a West Germanic language, he could very likely grasp the gist of the North Germanic poem, especially if it were written. The Eastern emperor in Constantinople could not read Caedmon's poem on the creation which Abbess Ethelfrith had read to her nuns at meals. Some of the nuns, on the other hand, had trouble with their Latin, so the abbess collected all the wholesome material she could in their vernacular, Old English (Anglo-Saxon), and had them copy it.

Languages change, like anything else of mankind. By 1200, Anglo-Saxon had become what we call Middle English; after 1400, the dialect of London gradually yields Modern or New English. Tolkien's mother's family, the Suffields, had lived in Evesham, Worcestershire, and would have spoken the West Midland dialect of Middle English. The orphan from South Africa attached himself to Worcestershire and always loved and studied its old speech.

During the Middle Ages, matter from many cultures was spreading from place to place, aided by Christian missionaries, Roman roads, and human desire for gain, whether by a fierce raid or by mutually beneficial commerce. Along with taxes, pilgrims, cloths, and spices traveled stories; material from various cultures got mixed, even mixed up. Icelanders were known to have good tales; so were Bretons, the Celtic people of Little Britain.[7] Many of the stories were in verse, which is easier for a reciter to carry in his mind than prose. In many long medieval narrative poems comes an obvious break, maybe due to mercy for the sitting-bones of its hearers. Also, if the bard, skald, or jongleur leaves them in suspense, they will have to keep him another night.

Many of the older poems are war stories, epic poems, based

(though with much embroidery) on a factual historical event, and celebrating a particular group of people. Other poems or songs, usually short, do not tell a story, but bring out one point or one feeling: Spring is come! or My purse is empty! or Night is Better than Day—No it isn't! or My Love is far away. These are lyric poems. And that last theme of love, which simply exploded in France, starting in Provence in the south early in the twelfth century, is a major contribution of the Middle Ages to the literature of the western hemisphere ever since.

The human race had been marrying, reproducing, caring, and generally active emotionally and sexually for some time previously, of course. But a new attitude comes to the foreground in the Middle Ages: the male lover uttering gasps of awe at his Lady, considering her his superior, his ruler, the one who elevates him. This attitude has come to be called courtly love. Where it came from is a question for lively debate. Some of the leading answers are: Islamic culture, classical culture, the cult of the Virgin Mary, and the circumstances of twelfth-century life.

The courtly lover is found in spring, in a garden, amid green leaves and flowerets of every hue. His hair is brushed, his nails are clean, but there are purple shadows under his eyes and his belt hangs on his hip-bones, for he has not been eating or sleeping; the thought of his Lady occupies his mind to the exclusion of all else, and he fears someone has been spreading rumors about him. He will not tell the Lady's name, but will describe her golden hair, beautiful figure, sweet voice, and graceful gait at length—unless she should appear. Then his voice will stick in his throat, his knees will quake, and he will sink to the ground. He will not notice Greek fire exploded under him, nor Noah's flood, nor the queen of that spring's tournament.

Story-poems written after this lyric explosion incorporated emotional interest, especially love, with adventurous material. Wartime settings were superseded by the adventures of an individual knight, often proving himself worthy of his Lady. Since one knows that the Middle Ages were the days of old when knights were bold, it comes as a shock to pick up pieces of real medieval literature and find them beginning, "Long ago in days of old when knights were bold. . . ."[8]

In places where the vernacular was a language descended from Latin but different, works in the vernacular were said to be written or recited "romanicē," as distinct from "latinē." The surge of vernacular tales of love and adventure has left us with the modern word romance, which twentieth-century English applies to all love stories; in European languages, the word often means "a novel."

Tolkien immersed himself gladly in the works of the medieval period, when languages were changing like the uplifting and weathering of mountains; and myth, folklore, legend, yarns, and art were voyaging from land to land, getting sung, getting lost, getting written, getting preserved.

III *Morris*

Partly because his name begins with *M*, William Morris (1834–1896) here represents the strain of nineteenth-century scholarship and imagination which forms Tolkien's immediate background; also because Morris deserves it. He was a diversely gifted man: he could write a book, design a typeface for it, print it, and sit down to read it in a reclining chair of his own design under wallpaper also his. He grieved that with the machines of mass production, people were losing joy in the things they made. Tolkien enjoyed his prose romances and fantasies. Morris too had been an Exeter College man.

He was part of a many-branched movement of the imagination, starting in the late eighteenth century, called romanticism. The name was given it, not with complimentary intentions, because among the things romantics enjoyed were romances from hundreds of years earlier, which the literary establishment of the day, Neoclassicism, considered crude and incredible.

C. S. Lewis has compared the romantic movement with the phenomenon of courtly love mentioned above. He suggests that in the twelfth century, Western culture was given a "picture" of a Lady to rouse and inspire it; in the late eighteenth, a picture of a landscape.

This landscape, let us say, is a towering cliff. Its feet plunge into the sea, whose colors differ in every weather and whose waves everlastingly break against the foot of the cliff, throwing spray high at the screaming gulls and flying clouds. Underneath are caves, inhabited by either a mermaid or a giant octopus. On the clifftop grow pink, salt-sprinkled flowers of thrift, low bushes from behind which deer dash away, and a single tree, probably an oak, bent to a fantastic shape by the eternal pressure of the seawind. Beneath this writhen oak—but hold, we go too fast.

Romanticism is usually defined, or at least its shape indicated, by setting it off against neoclassicism. In a nutshell, the difference is this: the classicist believes that the imposing of order by conscious effort, in any medium, produces beauty. Anyone who has looked at the Winged Victory carved out of marble rock or listened to a woodwind quartet will agree; so will those who admire lives of high discipline. The romantic believes that beauty occurs, and we must open ourselves to it wherever it finds us. Anyone who has looked at the inside of a geode or listened to a song sparrow will agree; so will those who admire lives of high emotion.

Back to yon writhen oak, beneath which broods, especially on stormy days, a lone man wrapped in a dark cloak, with one foot on the last stone of a lichen-crusted ruin. His hair is long, his chin unshaven. This is the romantic hero. His name, especially on stormy days, is Sensitive Accursed Me. If he will speak, he will talk about his loss, his illness, his travels, and what his strange vision portended. Do not let him walk too near the edge of the cliff, lest he do himself a mischief.

The neoclassic scene is the court of the king, who is doing his best to rule chesspieces emotionally affected by their own moves. A fountain is playing. Near it paces the neoclassic hero, a well-proportioned, clean-shaven young man with clear eyes, but at the moment a troubled brow. He has just learned from a messenger that fulfilling a family obligation, besides endangering his life, will wound the lady who is the object of his esteem. He needs time to think through his dilemma; lend him your ears and keep quiet while he reaches his decision to do his duty.

The romantics composed, painted, and wrote. They made up stories and adapted congenial old ones, such as the legend of Faust the magician, which Goethe worked into a mythic play. They also studied stories already written. Romances and epics

which had lain neglected for three hundred years and more
got pulled out of libraries, read, edited, and printed. Folktales
which country people and children's nurses had been retailing
got collected and written down, e.g., by Lönnrot in Finland
and notably by Jakob and Wilhelm Grimm in Germany.

The old tales were naturally written in old forms of the
language, so in nineteenth-century scholarship, philology holds
an important place (Greek, *philo-logos*, "lover of words"). This
same Jakob Grimm pieced together changes which had been
noticed in languages until he could joyfully demonstrate a regular rotation of consonants between his Germanic branch of the
Indo-European language family and the probable oldest form of
the language. Simplified, his law states that to shift a consonant
you blow through it and then you talk through it.[9] Where the
Grimms and English-speakers have *ff*athers, speakers of older
tongues had *pp*atres; where they and we eat *bb*eans, the ancients
ate *vv*avas; where we put stray animals in the *pp*ound, they
would have put them in a *bb*end. His description of this net-
work of regular consonant shifts is still called Grimm's Law: a
major stone in the edifice of philology.

Some of the stories made up in the romantic period leaped
to equality with the old folktales. We owe "Puss in Boots" to
Ludwig Tieck of Germany, "The Three Bears" to Robert Southey
of England, "The Ugly Duckling" and dozens more to Hans
Christian Andersen of Denmark.[10]

So Professor Tolkien, philologist, tale-spinner and mythmaker,
is not the Lonely Mountain. He is a peak in a range. But when
The Lord of the Rings was published, it struck its readers as
something the like of which had never been seen before. Why
was this so?

IV *Modern*

As aforesaid, neither publishers nor professors in general were
enthusiastic about fantasy during Tolkien's adulthood. They
were occupied by another literary movement: realism. It gathered strength round the middle of the nineteenth century and
is still with us.

The neoclassicist believes beauty comes from the conscious

imposing of order, and the romantic, that beauty occurs naturally; but the realist will not admit to seeking beauty at all.
Accuracy is his watchword. Stalk a realistic artist and you may
observe him giving order (like a classicist) to whatever un-
formed stuff he comes upon (like a romantic); but he would
not profess so much.

Neoclassical art does not tolerate mixtures. Romantic art loves
them. As the romantics say, mixtures occur in nature, so they
must be beautiful. Therefore a romantic play will mix the
comical with the tragic, and romantic fiction will gladly mix
the supernatural with the everyday. Classicists will shun both
the supernatural and the everyday and stick with the sublime.
Realists scorn the sublime, abjure the supernatural, and will
portray only the everyday.

The realistic hero, Tom, is crouching behind ashcans at the
foot of a wall in a bombed city. From the rickety bricks flutter
the shreds of a political poster. Somewhere a radio is blaring
a harsh tune. Tom scuttles away—he moves with a limp—but
slowly enough so you can follow him. He thinks you are from
the government and is leading you away from the basement
where he and Dick and Harry (Harry has three years of medical
school) and Geneviève have been living for six months. The
other three are there making a bomb, printing handbills, engaging in sexual intercourse, or shooting at the rats with someone's World War I pistol. The intestines must be wiped up
after every hit. If you catch up with the fugitive hero, offer him
a cup of cold water to drink: it is a sign of hope.

In the twentieth century, the ravages of war, then the ravages
of hysterical prosperity, then those of the international depression, and again world war, produced the certainty voiced by
narrators high and low, that the human race is in want of something. No one dares say what, nor how to find it. There is no
way out of the human condition,[11] though writers may show
small mitigations (see above, water).

In poetry, and influencing other genres, a big splash had been
made by T. S. Eliot's *Waste Land,* published in 1922, when he
was thirty-four. Both the form of the poem and its content
roused comment and respect; also puzzlement and dislike. Eliot's

view as he articulated it came to stand as the view of a generation. By the Waste Land, he meant the world he lived in.

> Here is no water but only rock
> Rock and no water and the sandy road
> The road winding above among the mountains
> Which are mountains of rock without water
> > T. S. Eliot, *The Waste Land*

Each section of the poem shows waste and abuses—mostly personal, often sexual—in that world. And in each section, while
drawing an ugly picture in broken lines, Eliot refers to rich
passages of myth and legend: the Holy Grail, Cleopatra, the
Rhine-gold—and then says he is using all this broken-apart lore
to prop up the shack he is living in, the orphaned prince of the
Waste Land.

Eliot, when he saw the world ugly, took care to use ugly
imagery to describe it:

> Let us go then, you and I,
> Where the evening is spread out against the sky
> Like a patient etherized upon a table.
> > "The Love Song of J. Alfred Prufrock"

Not everyone is pleased. Jack Lewis is moved to irony:

> For twenty years I've stared my level best
> To see if evening—any evening—would suggest
> A patient etherized upon a table;
> In vain. I simply wasn't able.
> To me each evening looked far more
> Like the departure from a silent, yet a crowded, shore
> Of a ship whose freight was everything, leaving behind
> Gracefully, finally, without farewells, marooned mankind.[12]

Lewis's feelings are not cheery, either; but his imagery is beautiful, as the evening sky looks to him. Here Eliot, the more
"modern" poet, shows something like the romantics' "pathetic
fallacy." He became happier as an Anglican.

With scarred Tom, Prufrock dodging his overwhelming question, the wasters of the Waste Land, and no author daring to

assert that he knew a way out of our misery, the literary world was far from expecting hobbits and rings, let alone the return of the king. More predictable was the *reductio ad absurdum* of the realistic movement: from realism, a frank, rounded portrayal of ordinary life; through naturalism, a frank portrayal of deliberately chosen ugliness, to the absurd: Tom limped from behind his ashcan; Nagg and Nell *live* in theirs.[13]

The literature of Europe and its heirs had followed a course all the way from the mythic to the ironic mode, as Northrop Frye puts it. Literature begins, he says, in the mythic mode, whose characters are demigods; next succeeds the romantic mode peopled by human beings superior to us; next, in the high mimetic mode, the characters are as good as us; in the low mimetic mode, as bad as us; finally, in the ironic mode, they are worse than us.[14] There was the mid-twentieth century, wallowed down in the ironic mode. Then *The Lord of the Rings* was published.

In truth, even in the days of Prufrock, Nagg, and Nell, the stream of fantasy was still running, like Kubla Khan's sacred river or Joseph Campbell's myth-hero, underground. Hope Mirlees was describing a stodgy little land beset by incursions from Faerie; E. R. Eddison, a student of Icelandic sagas, was chronicling wars, loves, and adventures on Mercury in a prose which sometimes broke through to the ultraviolet; Lord Dunsany was still writing his fantasies, touched sometimes with blood or humor, on what he called the marches between geography and fairyland; James Branch Cabell, happily using some conventions of realism and flouting others, was composing with rabelaisian verve a twenty-one-volume fantasy in the ironic mode which seduced even the critic Edmund Wilson.[15]

Fantasy was not dead, but as far as most people knew, it was in Limbo, waiting for the mythic horn blast to call it forth. Tolkien blew that blast.

CHAPTER 3

Playing and Thinking

Like Robert Frost's, Tolkien's "object in living is to unite / My avocation and my vocation, / As my two eyes make one in sight."

Robert Frost, "Two Tramps in Mud Time"

I Language

PEOPLE in their teens can do remarkable things. The new, full-sized bodies, fast keen minds, and energetic emotions of those years have powered battle leaders, merchants, and inventors. Often their capabilities are shown in the amassing of amounts of data incredible to people of other ages, be it sports-records or astronomy. Since human beings' intellects usually outpace their emotions in maturing, complicated factual material suits young people well. Nowadays, some memorize the genealogies of Middle-earth. It also suits them to gather with like-minded friends. An onlooker who was not like-minded would say they were working like galley slaves on their project, whatever it was. A sympathizer would recognize that they were playing—like galley slaves.

In these respects—a keen mind, a factual field of interest, and a group of congenial contemporaries—Tolkien was normal for his kind. A respect in which he was unusual, the emotional, served only to intensify his activities. As Carpenter points out, "At the age when many young men were discovering the charms of female company he was endeavoring to forget them and to push romance to the back of his mind."[1] Under force at eighteen to forego his beloved's company, even letters, until his majority, Tolkien—disinclined to fall for miscellaneous young ladies—applied himself all the harder to school, rugby, and especially language.

For language was his field of interest: languages and language.

41

A teenager who could dismantle and rebuild his Corvette with one hand might well quail at the thought of writing and delivering a speech in Gothic; Tolkien did it for a surprise during one of his school's Latin debates, acting a barbarian envoy. Gothic— the only East Germanic language, in which our only document of any length is a sixth-century silver-lettered Bible—was not a regular part of the curriculum at King Edward's School. Tolkien had picked it up himself from a copy of Wright's *Primer* discarded by a friend.

Tolkien's interest in languages had started before his teens. Tutored by his mother as a child in Sarehole, he had loved Latin. French had appealed to him less; bad experiences in France as an adult soured his attitude completely.[2] A bit of consolation for moving from Sarehole, when the Tolkien boys had to be nearer their school, was the coal cars on the railroad tracks below their window: they bore names the like of which Ronald had never seen before, names in Welsh! Speaking English, learning Latin, and being fascinated with Welsh put him in touch with three branches of Indo-European languages: Germanic, Italic, and Celtic. Father Morgan's Spanish, like French, is a Romance language; the Greek of King Edward's curriculum is Hellenic; and the Finnish he did some work with at Oxford is not an Indo-European language at all.

With stories, readers who like a particular kind will often try writing them. Tolkien has said that after reading a medieval text, he felt like writing one himself.[3] And he had the same reaction to language: after learning some, he devoted himself to making new ones. At first it was child's play for him and his cousins Mary and Marjorie Incledon. Especially with Mary, he worked their way from a rather primitive code to a language, Nevbosh (the New Nonsense). In the lonely years in rooms, he would work for hours on a better-designed language, Naffarin, based in some respects on Spanish. When he met the Finnish grammar, he used his gleanings from it in building a third language, his best-developed, Quenya. Like Finnish, Quenya can use one word for what in English would be a phrase, by putting endings onto a stem. "Fálmalïnnar," for example, means "upon many foaming waves."[4]

Tolkien studied languages extending not only halfway round

the globe in space, but also back some fifteen hundred years in time. At King Edward's he began on Middle English and was captivated not only because *Sir Gawain and the Green Knight* is a good story outstandingly told, but also because he realized that its language, the West Midland dialect, was that of his mother's ancestors. He loved the familiar because it was familiar and the strange because it was strange. Still encouraged by the English-master, Brewerton, he tracked back to Anglo-Saxon, also an ancestral tongue, though for a speaker of New English it takes a lot of learning. And then he met Anglo-Saxon's eastern cousin, Gothic.

For Gothic, as aforesaid, our documents are scarce. Tolkien found himself needing words for his speech which he did not have; they are not documented for that language. So he back-formed them: using languages he did know, and the laws of consonant and vowel shifts of which a good deal is known (e.g., Grimm's Law), the boy brought into being new Gothic words.

In his made-up languages, comparable processes took place under his hands. Sound-shifts in space: "The people across the river pronounce it oddly"; sound-shifts in time: "Grandpapa pronounces it oddly." And here he is caught. It might be possible to make up a language as a self-contained activity; but a *changing* language, which develops and branches, inescapably implies a history: Why are they across the river? Why does grandpapa sound funny to you? And a history, with a language, inescapably implies speakers: Who was across the river? Who is on this side? Who is my grandfather and who am I? Tolkien, willy-nilly, is going to be confronted with the task of making a world. And the idea—at least of chronicling a world—may not daunt him, at that.

By hindsight it appears that he was being led into becoming the Tolkien we know: unroller of the huge panorama of story detailed with the minutest gems of philological credibility.

By Providence, when this bright, philological, playful, rather lazy undergraduate went up to Oxford, there as the professor of philology was Joseph Wright, the very author of the Gothic primer which had caught the boy's imagination. Wright, growing up as a factory hand, had taught himself, then his fellows, to read and write. He became so fascinated that he went on to learn a dozen languages, earn a doctorate at Heidelberg, and settle with a like-minded wife at England's great university.

Tolkien, the supposed classics major, got a B on his classical exams ("moderations" or "mods"), but a high A in philology. Recognizing where his true interest lay, he changed his major to the language branch of the English School, and in 1915 took his degree with first class honors: an A.

When Tolkien first changed his major, he looked over the syllabus of his new department and sighed inwardly: was *that* supposed to keep him mentally busy for two years? He had learned Middle English and read the best of its literature in school, and the same for Anglo-Saxon. But he had not yet read the Advent poem *Crist*, by Cynewulf. In it appears a line which electrified Tolkien: "Hail, Earendel, brightest of angels, over middle-earth sent to men."

The word "middle-earth" poses no problem: it is a Germanic expression for the world of men. In this mythology, our world is washer shaped. Inside is Asgard, the home of the gods. Outside (so ours is "middle") round the ring are worlds of fire, frost, trolls, giants, etc. About "Earendel," Tolkien's best guess was that the name hailed the Morning Star and was used by Cynewulf to refer to John the Baptist, precursor of Christ. But from now on, the image of *Earendel, engla beorhtast / ofer middangeard monnum sended* was working in his mind, along with certain other bits of mythology.

II   Beowulf: the Monsters and the Critics

Tolkien had read the poem *Beowulf* in school, both in translation and in the original Anglo-Saxon. But of course it was on the Oxford syllabus, being the monument of Anglo-Saxon literature and indeed one of the world's. It was written down about 1000 A.D., but seems to reflect a state of things more like the sixth century, with matter which later learned people consider wholly legendary.

In the first section of the poem, the young hero Beowulf arrives at the gilded hall of the Danish king, which is invaded by the monster Grendel. Beowulf boasts of having killed a family of sea-monsters, tears Grendel apart, and kills his mother at the bottom of her pool. In the second part, fifty years later, Beowulf as an old king faces a dragon who is menacing his subjects. He tells his thanes to let him advance alone, and when he needs help, only young Wiglaf dares go to him. The dragon is killed, but so is Beowulf. His people build a pyre by the sea, and ride round it singing of his nobility and love of glory.

Rereading *Beowulf* at Oxford, Tolkien got more out of it, as one does on second readings. Twenty-odd years later, as a professor, he gave a lecture on it to the British Academy: *Beowulf: the Monsters and the Critics*, a landmark in *Beowulf* criticism. He opens by prettily and aptly mocking his predecessors for two main mistakes: first, regarding this poem only as evidence— historical, philological, or whatever. Anyone using *Beowulf* so was overlooking its being a piece of art, and therefore was no critic. The second mistake was reading *Beowulf* as a poem, indeed, but finding it defective by the critic's criteria, which he had never lined up with the poet's criteria. Tolkien, a connoisseur of dragons from childhood, was especially irked by other readers being irked by the centrality of the monsters in *Beowulf*. Wild folk elements, they called them; and of course the fantastic was childish. Such allegations would of course draw out Tolkien, as mad as a plundered dragon.

With a flash he illuminates a wide view, showing us the *Beowulf*-poet at work; forty years later we see that the poet's shape is Tolkien's shape, at work upon *The Silmarillion*. No, says the lecturer of the 1930s, the monsters have not usurped the center of the poem, and the historical material used as trimming is *meant* for trimming. The story claims truth rather than factuality. By means of the monsters, and merely supported by the history, the poet makes the poem what he wants it to be: a picture of man on earth. Man on earth is doomed in time. To show this at its clearest, the Christian poet has set his poem in his people's heroic pagan past: days he realizes were "heathen, noble, and hopeless." Heroism is remembered and sung, but can gain for the hero and his people at most a respite before the next attack, never salvation.

III   *The Homecoming of Beorhtnoth Beorhthelm's Son*

The matter of heroism, what constituted it and what good it did, was much on Tolkien's mind. He had read bygone ages' heroic poetry, and then been in a real, messy war, with officers above him and men below. Danger held no glamor for him. A danger can kill; and if the hero does not overcome the danger, it will proceed to injure more people, whether the danger be a troll, a lie, or the *sales Boches*.

Beowulf and *Sir Gawain and the Green Knight* deal with this concern.[5] More tantalizingly, because the poem is incomplete, so does *The Battle of Maldon*, an Anglo-Saxon work written close to the date of the battle it records, 991. The great old Earl Beorhtnoth had an invasion of vikings to stand off. They had landed on an island and were contained there, but asked Beorhtnoth to let them over the causeway at low tide to fight a pitched battle. He agreed. He was killed, and all his trusty companions fighting round him. The vikings—this is not in the poem—sailed off and took ten thousand pounds from other towns along the coast.

The dying words of Beorhtnoth's old retainer Beorhtwold, near the end of our fragment, express to perfection the Northern heroic ethos: "Heart shall be bolder, harder be purpose, / more proud the spirit as our power lessens!" These lines are famous, and Tolkien's friend E. V. Gordon recognized *Maldon* as second only to *Beowulf* among Old English heroic poetry. But Tolkien noticed especially two other lines (89f.), which criticize the earl's pride in letting the enemy step onto his land: he acted in *ofermod*, an excess of spirit (cf. New English, "overtired," "overworked").

It would be fitting for Professor Tolkien to write an article on the question of glory versus foolishness in battle. But Tolkien was not quite the man to do that. His professorial works seldom saw print, because for every matter which interested him enough to write an article, he wanted to do, needed to do, more. For *The Battle of Maldon* he did write an article, published in 1953; but he had done more, according to that inner urge: he had continued *Maldon* (in New English, using the old verse form) with a scene of Beorhtnoth's followers recovering his body on the field. By the eyes of the young minstrel Torhthelm and the middle-aged farmer Tidwald, Tolkien could look briefly round the question of heroism and chivalry. Torhthelm, his mind full of Grendels and Beowulfs, finds their master's headless body "mangled with axes. What murder it is, / this bloody fighting!" Tidwald, who regards the youth with good-natured irony, makes the point, "Aye, that's battle for you, / and no worse today than wars you sing of. . . . / The world wept then, as it weeps today: / you can hear the tears through the harp's twanging."[6] Tolkien's poem, "The Homecoming of Beorhtnoth Beorhthelm's Son," seemed so effective that the BBC took it for a radio play in 1954.[7]

IV *On Fairy Stories*

In theory, drama was not Tolkien's genre, though all through his life he was getting involved in plays, skits, and theatricals for fun. He also respected drama's ability to show the doom of man in this world. But his great devotion was to pure narrative, to story. This he stated most clearly in "On Fairy Stories," his Andrew Lang lecture in 1939, in the series named for the folklorist-collector of the colored Fairy Books, which Tolkien had read as a child.

A way to get Tolkien's views out in public was to make him give a lecture: then he had to gather his thoughts, put them into form—he had been a debater in school—and present them at a certain time. *Beowulf: the Monsters and the Critics* and "On Fairy Stories" are in fact his major nonfictional works, both originally speeches.

From childhood, fairy stories were among his reading; to the end of his life (and still) he would receive brickbats from people considering such interests unbefitting a grown professor. People's taste may not be converted by a lecture, but "On Fairy Stories" proves even to those who will never agree with it that a love of Faerie need not involve decayed or immature mental faculties; the lecture is lively and clear.

Tolkien considers whether fairy tales, which he had loved increasingly—and been writing, though only the juvenile *Hobbit* had been published—whether such tales have in the real world

or real universe the value which his heart tells him they have.
He concludes that fairy tales, best of all literature, offer four
values: fantasy, the making by artist-man of something which
was not in the primary world; recovery, a fresh appreciation of
the things in the primary world; escape, a mental vacation away
from hard and ugly places and times; and consolation, the lift
of the heart we receive from a happy ending. Tolkien calls this
inspiriting kind of ending a *eucatastrophe* (Greek, "good turning"), a word which deserves wider adoption.

After hesitating at his presumption, Tolkien observes that at
one point, the lines of myth and history seem to have crossed:
with the life of Jesus. That is, material well-known round the
globe in mythology is reported to have happened at a verifiable
point in space and time. The happy surprise of death defeated,
what Beowulf could not do, is soberly announced from Jerusalem. Tolkien takes this real story, God's creation, for a sign
(among its other significances) that artist-man's making of such
eucatastrophic tales is one of his blessed activities.

Part of "On Fairy Stories" comes from a conversation with
Hugo Dyson and C. S. Lewis one windy autumn night in 1931.
Lewis loved narrative, myth, and especially Norse myth; but
because mythology is not factual, he called it lies. Tolkien and
Dyson jumped on him and started trying to show how Lewis
erred. The poem Tolkien afterward wrote him, which he quotes
in "On Fairy Stories," began what he enlarges in the lecture,
his idea about subcreation, summed up in the preface to this
book.

It was a rare occasion, this lecture in which Tolkien spoke
openly about his religious beliefs. They formed a vital part of
his thinking, but were a part of his iceberg which he kept
submerged, in contrast to Lewis, Anglicanism's most articulate
and prolific spokesman of the century. Tolkien was, as aforesaid, a devout Roman Catholic. But his fiction has made various impressions and roused conflicting comments. He has been
panned for having no religion and praised for having no religion. His morality has been called black-and-white, contrived,
subtle, realistic. He has been charged with upholding "the
Anglican doctrine of predestination" when he was not an
Anglican—and neither Anglicans nor Romans believe in pre-

destination! Come to find out, the speaker meant the Christian doctrine of Providence. Outward practices such as Westerners nowadays associate with religion are certainly absent in his fiction, for reasons examined in chapter 5. Yet some Catholics, after reading *The Lord of the Rings* in 1955, felt certain he was a Catholic, because of the tale's ambiance, and he was. In "On Fairy Stories," his thinking on literary art led him to be explicit, for once, about being a follower of Jesus, Whom he believed to be eucatastrophe incarnate for this world and for humankind.

V   The Adventures of Tom Bombadil

Tolkien, though slow in producing major writings, liked to grace social occasions with spirited short works. At Leeds and at Oxford, he would coin into skillful verse his feelings on the doorstep of an Exalted Academic Person, or the survival of Michael's doll which John had stuffed down the toilet.[8] Or the professor would take a fragment of old lore and attempt to discover the history and social conditions which underlay it: specifically, he would expand nursery rhymes. Our familiar "Hey Diddle Diddle" and "The Man in the Moon" are enigmatic verses, if one chooses to look at them so. Tolkien in scholarly fashion has "restored" a coherent form of the story.[9]

His old Aunt Jane asked in 1961 if he would not publish something about Tom Bombadil, affordable for Christmas presents; so he gathered a handful of these poems of the 1920s and 1930s, plus a couple of new ones, added a mock-scholarly introduction, and we have *The Adventures of Tom Bombadil.* Fortunately, he had moved promptly for once; Jane Neave died less than a year after it was printed.

Enamored as he was of beautiful and skilful patterns, and working as he did with words, of course Tolkien wrote poetry. Even in his prose, lines turn up like bits of song: "In winter here no heart could mourn for summer or for spring" (I, 454). As a speaker of New English, he found himself a uniquely rich heir both in words and in traditions of versification.

Classical verse was patterned by its arrangement of long and short syllables, in little groups called "feet": note the implied association of patterned words with the patterned movement of the dance.[10] As classical Latin became Vulgar (i.e., common) Latin, which in turn became the Romance languages, its verse began to be patterned by regularly recurring endings: rhyme. Neighboring non-Romance languages liked the sound and adopted rhyme too; Goethe's *Faust* (part 2) has a scene of the German magician teaching Helen of Troy this new wordplay.

But older Germanic verse had not patterned itself by rhyme, nor by feet. Instead of regular syllable-groups, its lines had a regular count of stressed syllables (corresponding to though not the same as classical long ones), but varying numbers of unstressed. And for regularly recurring sounds, instead of rhyme (sneeze, freeze, disease), older Germanic verse used alliteration (freeze, friend, afraid) within the line. Tolkien uses the *Beowulf* meter in "The Homecoming of Beorhtnoth": four stresses, two or three of them alliterating, with a break (caesura) in the middle of the line.[11]

The meter of Tolkien's two Bombadil poems is the same as Tom speaks for most of his conversation in *The Fellowship of the Ring*, though there it is written as prose. It is like the meter of a sixteenth-century "Song of Robin Goodfellow."[12] The lines, varying Anglo-Saxonly in their count of unstressed syllables, are mostly heptameters, often with a dactyl before the caesura, rhyming in couplets *a a b b c c*, etc. Some lines in "Bombadil Goes Boating" and many in "The Adventures" are hexameters. The rhymes are all feminine: ending in an unstressed syllable (fellow/yellow, take you/make you). Some lines show a characteristic feature of Tolkien's poetry: extra spondees (consecutive stressed syllables):

He *wore* in his *tall hat* a *swan-wing fea*ther (*ATB*, 11).

Tolkien speaks of Bilbo's having invented the metrical tricks in "Errantry" and being "proud of them" (*ATB*, 8); the same form is used in Bilbo's serious poem about Earendil (I, 308ff.). Tolkien means himself, of course. The meter, iambic tetrameter, is an enduring war-horse, but the rhyme scheme is of exquisite difficulty: all on double-feminine endings, with an internal rhyme (at least approximate) between the end of every other line and the middle of the next.

> He passed the archipelagoes
> where yellow grows the marigold,
> where countless silver fountains are,
> and mountains are of fairy-gold.

> (*ATB*, 25)

Tolkien obviously loved wrestling with such word challenges; small wonder his writing took so long. Some people take string and make cat's cradles. One wonders whether Tolkien tried to write the serious poem first and kept finding the words dishing him up a parody:

> He made a shield and morion
> of coral and of ivory,
> a sword he made of emerald. . . .

> (*ATB*, 25)

Kocher points out the impracticability of such armament, of which Tolkien would also be aware.[13]

It is unknown whether "Princess Mee" began from Priscilla's noticing an equally pretty child in the mirror. At any rate, her father tries to reflect the phenomenon of reflection in words:

> With pearls in hair
> And kirtle fair
> And slippers frail
> Of fishes' mail went Mee:
> Of fishes' mail
> And slippers frail
> And kirtle fair
> With pearls in hair went Shee!

> (*ATB*, 30)

"The Stone Troll" originally came out as "The Root of the Boot" in *Songs for Philologists,* a batch of ditties by Tolkien and some colleagues at Leeds.[14] The present version is tightened up, in that the refrain words now relate to the story as well as sustaining the rhythm and rhyme. Tolkien would be the last to claim the crown of poetry for his light verses; but their vigor and appropriateness make them stick in the mind. Who could forget the hobbits' bath song (I, 145) when happy in a hot tub?

"Perry-the-Winkle" recounts a situation similar to "The Dragon's Visit":[15] a wild creature of legend appears in a snug smug village. "The Dragon's Visit" involves bloodshed and a warrior-maid; but in "Perry-the-Winkle" benefits accrue all round because one petty person has the courage to practice charity.

Tolkien gives us three poems of bestiary lore, a fascinating branch of medieval studies.[16] "Cat," with its triple internal rhymes, alliterations, and assonances, shows us the philologist juggling his treasures again.

The last four poems in the book shift to a serious tone; two are clear, two enigmatic. The man in "Shadow-Bride" seems to be in the predicament of Chamisso's Peter Schlemiehl, and to find a solution; as the lady dances with him, we can guess that she agrees to joining him.

"The Hoard" was originally entitled with a line from *Beowulf*, "Iumonna Gold Galdre Bewunden," or "The gold of the men of old, entwined with a spell" (l. 3052). Thinking of this and presumably of Fafnir's hoard, as well as the treasure of Nargothrond in his own mythology, Tolkien writes a short but concentrated meditation on one of his major themes: greed. The spondees and masculine rhymes help to convey a sense of the unhurried but inevitable approach of doom toward the possessive.

Tolkien says "The Sea-Bell" is tagged "Frodos Dreme" (*ATB*, 9); it may have been one of Tolkien's own. The style is still characteristic of Tolkien's poetry, but here is overshadowed by the strange tale. It is an anxious dream: a quest-story which does not come off. Rather than separation, initiation, and return, the dreamer goes on a journey, but is shunned at his destination and on his coming home as well. He finds nothing and brings back nothing, and nobody cares. Though Tolkien's account of the dream is eerily beautiful, the dream shows fear and frustration.[17]

But in real life, Tolkien, who had been to a strange land in his mind, *was* able to share his experiences with a great many people, although he never personally met most of them. Tolkien in "On Fairy Stories," and many Tolkienists after him, have emphasized that he dislikes a good deal about our century (e.g., motorcars); this is partly why he sets his stories in the far past. Roger Sale carries Tolkien's "escape of the prisoner" (rather than "flight of the deserter") image a step farther by pointing out that Tolkien was not just fleeing *from* something he disliked, but *to* something he was discovering with love.[18] The next step is to realize that Tolkien, an authentic contemporary quest-hero, has completed all three steps of a successful quest: he has *gone, found,* and *returned* with trove for us.

"The Last Ship" is a very Tolkienian elegiac piece on the fading of an age of wonder and the abandonment of the human race to a stodgy existence. He seems to have mulled the question all his life: when beauty is so beautiful, what worth can stodginess have? Firiel's brown dress, chores, and braided hair at the end of the poem contrast painfully with the elves in their swan-drawn boat. Only in Tolkien's maturest work does he achieve a balance among beauty, mortality, and stodginess: elves, human beings, and hobbits; and who plays the most important part may have surprised even the author.

VI Farmer Giles of Ham

Stories fascinated Tolkien; broken bits of stories fascinated him; and of course words fascinated him, especially names. His philologist's mind would tease and worry at interesting words until he had an explanation which was either true or irresistible. Driving in the 1930s round Oxfordshire and neighboring Buckinghamshire, he would come to the villages of Thame and Worminghall, pronounced Tame and Wunnle. Of course the Tolkien imagination could never let that situation rest. A worm was a snake, or indeed a dragon. A dragon at a hall? Tamed? How could that have come about? And if Thame meant tame, how did the *h* get there, its incongruity underlined by the name of Aich Hill, rising above the village?[19]

A dragon broods on gold, like avarice incarnate. They cannot be tamed but must be killed. Who can kill a dragon? A hero. It will very likely cost him his life, like Beowulf; or leave him with a permanent curse, like Sigurd who took Fafnir's treasure; or the dragon's gold will tame the hero into a greedy old shadow,

as in Tolkien's "The Hoard"(*ATB*, 53). As noted before, Tolkien
does not completely trust the warrior-hero.

Yet the village names spoke to him of a tame worm. Who
might tame one? Maybe an Englishman such as Tolkien had
come to admire soldiering in the war and studying at Leeds:
a person basically unassuming, but shrewd; caring nothing for
chivalry, but brave if forced to be so either by embarrassment
or by others' danger. Thus Tolkien arrived at the character of
Farmer Giles of Ham, whose name means "red-bearded de-
fender of the village" (or "of the pasture"). The word Ham—
Tolkien's explanation is found—must be the source of the intru-
sive *h* in Thame.

A man like Giles might tame a worm. But, Tolkien realized
further, a worm who could be tamed would be a different reptile
from the Fafnir of his childhood reading or the Smaug—let alone
Glaurung—of his adult writing. His imagination worried the
problem. Treasure, malice—and death: these are the associa-
tions of dragons: not tameness. However, great love of treasure
is well known to debase the character. In a time when knights—
even the king—had become petty and vacillating,[20] might not
one of the dragon-breed have gone the same way? A lover of
treasure, yes, but an even greater lover of his own skin? So
Tolkien gives us Chrysophylax (Greek, "guardian of gold"),
whose sense of self-preservation outweighs his dragonish greed
and guile. The sword in *Farmer Giles of Ham*, Caudimordax or
Tailbiter, bears an old dragon-name; it translates the Greek
Ouroboros.[21]

In writing *Farmer Giles of Ham*, Tolkien was doing tongue-
in-cheek what some medieval and biblical stories do seriously:
explaining the origins of given place-names. Often the origin-
legends are not plausible, being based on misunderstandings or
folk etymologies. For instance, in *The Mabinogion*, the story of
Branwen includes a memorable explanation of the place-name
Talebolion, understood as "payment of colts"; but scholars nowadays think it probably means "end of the ridges."[22]

Tolkien told "Farmer Giles" to his family and showed it to
Allen and Unwin, but as it was not about hobbits they did not
publish it. Tolkien read an expanded version to a student club
at Oxford, who broke up laughing. In 1949 Allen and Unwin

did print the story, paper being available again after the war. To illustrate it they found Pauline Baynes, who went on to illustrate Lewis's Narnia chronicles and Tolkien's *Adventures of Tom Bombadil* and *Smith of Wootton Major*.

VII *Leaf by Niggle*

Tolkien, like every writer, longs to show his readers "how it is"; writers of fiction too, though their "how it is" is refracted through the story's "how it was" or "how it would be if." To convey one's sense of how it is is difficult, especially if more than facts is involved. More is nearly always involved: probably at least two sets of facts and at least one charge of emotion. We perceive emotion the most intensely, yet have the hardest time conveying it.

To do so successfully, one wants an echo of the emotion to resonate in the reader. Abstract words notoriously do not resonate; concrete, sense-touching words can. T. S. Eliot puts it so:

The only way of expressing emotion in the form of art is by finding "an objective correlative"; in other words, a set of objects, a situation, a chain of events which shall be the formula for that *particular* emotion; such that when the external facts, which terminate in sensory experience, are given, the emotion is immediately evoked.[23]

For instance, Eliot does not say, "I consider my portion of space-time impoverished and sinister, and I feel afraid and discouraged." He says, "I think we are in Rats' Alley, where the dead men lost their bones." Now his readers can share some of his feelings.

A writer strives to make facts and feelings clear to his readers —and also to himself. A person is only partly clear in his conscious mind how the world seems to him; that is one reason people need to dream. Dreams have mattered in Tolkien's life: it was on waking one morning in 1943 or early 1944 that he found the short story "Leaf by Niggle" in his mind, wrote it down, and read it to Edith.

The story was an "objective correlative" for his state of mind. With no autobiographical facts in it—in one sense—it tells a

great deal about what it was like to be J. R. R. Tolkien, and even
about the condition and hope of the human race, as refracted
through Tolkien's mind.

Niggle is an artist who will have to go on a journey, but he
never does any packing or tidying. He works on a painting
which began as a leaf, which turned out to be on a tree, which
turned out to stand in a landscape. . . . Niggle is repeatedly
interrupted by his lame neighbor Parrish, who sometimes gives
him home-grown potatoes. One rainy night when Parrish's roof
leaks—he eyes Niggle's painted canvas jealously—Niggle must
ride his bicycle for the doctor for Mrs. Parrish. After this he is
summoned on his journey. Some townspeople speak slightingly
of the departed and take the canvas to patch the roof.[24] One
saves a leaf.

Niggle, lacking baggage, is sent to the Workhouse, where he
must do certain chores for certain periods. He becomes handy
at using, rather than pottering away, time. Then he hears two
august Voices discussing his case; the second recommends
Gentle Treatment.

Niggle is taken on a train-ride to a hill, over whose crest he
finds his tree and all the country beyond. "It's a gift!" he cries.
But for gardening the country to its full beauty, he finds he
needs Parrish, who thereupon arrives. The two tend the land
until Niggle feels the urge to go on to the distant mountains.
The story ends with both men, now in the mountains, learning
that the place with the tree has been named Niggle's Parish.
"Laughed—the Mountains rang with it!"

Tolkien's dreaming mind, like everyone's dreaming mind but
with unusual coherence, has given him a concrete image of how
things are in his feelings, thoughts, and hopes. Niggle's work
of art, the tree, is doing just what Tolkien's work of art, *The
Lord of the Rings,* was doing: growing with what seems like
an authority of its own from a compact, manageable idea to a
whole which is coherent, but so vast as to seem almost infinite
to the artist chasing his runaway brain-child.[25]

Tolkien, having passed his half-century, though still hale,
knew he would not live forever. Like Niggle, he would have to
go. He had always been poignantly conscious of this aspect of
the human condition, as mentioned in chapter 1. But as a story-

teller, he sensed the life of this world as profoundly dissatisfying if it were the only state for human beings: it has loose ends. And Tolkien was the lecturer of "On Fairy Stories," who had claimed that human art can reflect the way things are in primary (God's) creation.

About the life of this world we know, because we live it; and about the final state of a person we have heard from religion: the human race is made to be with its Creator, "in Heaven" as we say, thinking in terms of space. A person can also end in the "place" which wants no God, "in Hell." But artistically, the jump from this world to Heaven or Hell is rarely satisfying; and the human artistic sense, says Tolkien, comes from God. Then may our restless imaginations think of other states besides Earth, Heaven, and Hell? Yes, replies Tolkien's Catholic faith. Though God *can* get camels through needles' eyes (or camels with packs on through Needle-eye Gate), we need not imagine Niggle with all his self-absorptions and lazinesses upon him precipitated into the Creator's direct presence.

There can be an intermediary state: Purgatory, the cleaning place. Dante, our greatest storyteller of the afterlife, makes Purgatory a mountain rooted near the feet of Hell, rising to the outskirts of Paradise. Holy-card pictures of Tolkien's time would show people chest-deep in flames, naked and sad-faced but not ugly, raising their eyes and chained hands toward a blue sky: the "poor souls" in a static, passive state of suffering and waiting. People living in this world were urged to pray and do good works on their behalf.

The church somewhat discourages speculation about lives after this world, since (1) we cannot really imagine them; (2) this world is our business while we are in it; (3) preoccupation with other spheres can easily become unwholesome.[26] Nevertheless, people's minds will occupy themselves with the question, waking or sleeping. "Leaf by Niggle" is Tolkien's little *Purgatorio*; and with its writing, with the externalizing in concrete pictures of Tolkien's worries, his writing of *The Lord of the Rings* came unstuck and proceeded relatively fast for several months. C. S. Lewis was working on a *Purgatorio* at the same time, published in 1946 as *The Great Divorce*.[27]

Tolkien's dreaming mind, in presenting him with "Leaf by

Niggle," did something his conscious mind would never do: used allegory. Awake, Tolkien says, "I cordially dislike allegory in all its manifestations, and always have done so since I grew old and wary enough to detect its presence" (I, vii). In his introduction to the *Pearl*, he distinguished between allegory and its relative, symbolism: "it is useful to limit allegory to narrative, to an account (however short) of events; and symbolism to the use of visible signs or things to represent other things or ideas. . . . But an allegorical description of an event [e.g., death as journey] does not make that event itself allegorical."[28] He also says, "I think that many confuse 'applicability' with 'allegory'; but the one resides in the freedom of the reader, and the other in the purposed domination of the author" (I, xi). Tolkien dislikes the allegorizing author's trying to dominate the reader; but in sleep, he was not even trying to dominate himself. His mind, feeling powerfully that death is like a journey and a work of art like a growing tree, presents him with concrete images in a coherent narrative, as if he too were a reader. The story, like a dream, may be taken at face value, or mulled over and interpreted.

VIII   Smith of Wootton Major

Tolkien's other published short story, *Smith of Wootton Major*, arose from a conscious attempt to tell how it is, "it" this time being a magical imagination. His lecture on mankind's imagination, "On Fairy Stories," had been reprinted in 1964, and he was becoming widely recognized as having a unique imagination himself. So a publisher asked him to write a preface for "The Golden Key" and other short stories by George Macdonald. Tolkien had enjoyed Macdonald's *Princess and the Goblin* and *The Princess and Curdie* as a child. But on reading or rereading the short stories, he was saddened and annoyed. They trivialized their material, Tolkien felt: they were prettified, they were saccharine, they seemed like—like a very sweet cake with a dolly fairy on the icing. So he started a story to illustrate his preface, but the preface got shucked off like a chrysalis and the story emerged as *Smith*: a tale not only of mankind's magical imagination, but of Tolkien and his imagination and old age; he was now in his seventies.

In the story, a cake is served every twenty-four years at the Feast of Good Children: the supreme test of the Master Cook. The cook Noakes has some notions about sweetness and decoration—fairies are good for kids—but leaves most of the work to his apprentice, Alf.

Always watch names. "Alf" suggests a lower-class lad, but the word is the same as "elf."

Among the trinkets to bake in the cake a star turns up, which Alf calls a fay-star. It is swallowed by young Smith, who begins to show unusual grace in his singing, and when he grows up, in his ironwork. He becomes friendly with Alf, and sometimes he travels to Faery where he meets adventures small and great. "There is *no* allegory in the Faery, which is conceived as having a real extra-mental existence," Tolkien wrote.[29] As another Feast of Good Children draws near, Smith realizes he should put the star back into the cake; with a wrench he does so. Alf Prentice, now the Master Cook, to whom Smith hands over the star, turns out to be the King of Faery. His time has come to leave the village. Again, Tolkien shows the passing of a blessed time, whose blessing was unrecognized while present.

Tolkien read *Smith* to his family and sent it to his publishers, who called on Pauline Baynes to illustrate it and issued it as a small book in 1967.[30]

IX *Other Arts*

Writing is so outstandingly Tolkien's craft that his activity in other arts could be overlooked. He was no mean draftsman, especially in portraying places. *The Hobbit* was printed with his paintings and drawings. *The Father Christmas Letters*, printed posthumously in full color, show him having great fun with pens and paints, lights and darkness. "You can't paint fizzing light, can you?" he writes, attempting fireworks.[31] Some of his pictures and inscriptions have been printed in calendars and as covers to the Ballantine paperbacks, replacing artwork which had stung him to indignation when he first saw it.[32] Christopher, still editing, brought out the calendar pictures in a sumptuous book in 1979.

Tolkien has even contributed to the music of his secondary world. Donald Swann, of the musical wits Flanders and Swann, composed settings for several songs from Middle-earth. When he showed Tolkien his draft of a tune for "Namarië" (Galadriel's Lament), the author objected. He sang Swann a phrase like Gregorian chant, explaining that in his own mind, he heard the song that way. Swann recognized the theme's suitability and incorporated it into his song-cycle, *The Road Goes Ever On.*[33]

Throughout Tolkien's life, playing and thinking, he was always setting in order through art the things which most attracted him, amused him, or worried him. He built sounds into languages, words into histories, and periods of sadness into tales with hope.

CHAPTER 4

For His Children

TOLKIEN had read the world's stories and entered into the
workings of language. These two mental endowments
formed a foundation for his extracurricular work; one sees why
a person with such interests could spend hours on private languages and even a private mythology. But Tolkien's works have
not remained private. Drawn out though the process has been,
he has written them down, shown them to other people, and
let them be printed. It seems that he was able to do this because,
at each stage of his career, he had the encouragement of living
people to hear what he was saying. Along with his love of
stories and of language, his audiences gave the necessary third
element for his becoming the author we know.

At King Edward's School his chief audience was the Tea Club
and Barrovian Society, to which Carpenter has given due promi-
nence. During his years with his schoolmates Wiseman, Smith,
and Gilson, Tolkien first conceived the idea of writing a mythology for England. He committed some of his strong impressions
—the Cornish sea, the star Earendel—to poetry, which he showed
to these friends. They did not stand in awe of him, as the Inklings and his children also did not in his later life. Wiseman on
reading the poems wrote to Tolkien that he was reminded of a
poet compared "to a lady who liked to put on all her jewelry
after breakfast. Don't overdo it."[1] All his key audiences combined what a writer needs most, love and stringency.

The four young men of the T.C.B.S. felt made for something
special. During World War I, Smith wrote to Tolkien, "if I am
scuppered tonight . . . there will still be left a member of the
great T.C.B.S. to voice what I dreamed and we all agreed
upon. . . . may you say the things I have tried to say long after
I am not there to say them, if such be my lot."[2] Smith's lot was

61

death. As the war drew to its end, Wiseman prodded Tolkien,
"You ought to start the epic."[3]

He started it. His company now was his young wife Edith,
who heard early tales from what became the late-published
work, *The Silmarillion*. She encouraged his thinking along fairy-
tale lines, as she loved "spring and flowers and trees and little
elfin people."[4] Spring, flowers, and trees her husband loved too,
to the end of his days. His tolerance got lower and lower for
"little elfin people," with all the trivial prettiness implied in
"elfin."[5] The adjective pertaining to his elves, as his typesetters
were repeatedly admonished, is *elven*.

After he and Edith had the children, a new kind of audience
was there for Tolkien. Children have a huge appetite for being
told things, both factual and fanciful. Their experience is limited,
their feelings usually more in need of calming than of rousing.
Their criticism of a work—usually questions about it—bears on
the matter in hand, not abstractions from it; and the questions
are not, as adults' may be, meant merely to show off the capac-
ities of the questioner.

Tolkien, having grown up without his father, was interested
in his relationship with his children. His third son, Christopher,
turned out to be especially congenial. John, the oldest, was the
first recipient of Tolkien's stories; when he could not sleep, his
father would spin yarns of a boy called Carrots. And when
Michael had nightmares, he was consoled with accounts of the
crimes of Bill Stickers and his pursuit by Major Road. Once
Michael lost a toy dog: a situation such as has driven many a
parent to storytelling, either to say the toy is all right or to show
another child in the same trouble. Tolkien saved the situation
with "Roverandom," a well-received story of a dog involved
with wizards, a trip to the Moon, and a dragon. Michael's Dutch
doll Tom Bombadil (the object of John's hostility) inspired a
couple of starts at stories and eventually gained a small but vivid
part in the history of the Ring.

During the 1930s, the Tolkiens had a motorcar, their vehicle
for visiting Thame, Worminghall, the barrow called Wayland's
Smithy, and other places round Oxford.[6] The professor was not
a particularly prudent nor skilful driver. And he observed, long
before it became a matter of wide public concern, the damage

done by motors multiplying unchecked; so that even after the end of World War II's gas rationing, the family did not get another car. Bicycles are more practical in Oxford anyway.[7] Tolkien penned satires on the motorworks near Oxford, disparaged them in "On Fairy Stories," and for the children wrote "Mr. Bliss," based on his own misadventures. He completed the story and illustrated it in color, but it remains unpublished in the archives at Marquette University in Milwaukee.

Starting when John was three and Michael newborn, Tolkien had an annual game: sending the children a letter from Father Christmas. Children's letters to Santa Claus had long been common; Tolkien's special kind of imagination, humor, and fatherliness dictated replies. The custom continued until after the outbreak of World War II, when Priscilla, the youngest Tolkien child, was ten. The envelopes bore stamps and meticulous postmarks; postage was two kisses. Some years the Oxford mailman cooperated in delivering the letters.[8]

Father Christmas lives at the North Pole, as contemporary folklore dictates. It is a pole; Tolkien could scarcely resist a pun. He endowed Father Christmas with a comic sidekick, the North Polar Bear, Karhu (Finnish, "bear"); and later with elf assistants, one of whom became his secretary: Ilbereth. All three wrote distinctive hands, and Karhu invented an alphabet somewhat reminiscent of Sherlock Holmes's dancing men.

Karhu is principally a bungler. He breaks the North Pole, wastes two years' worth of aurora in a night (that is what caused Tolkien's difficulties drawing "fizzing light"), and leaves his bathwater overflowing. But he also fights heroically against Goblins. He "is a very MAGICAL animal really, and Goblins can't do much to him" (last letter).

Goblins appear at the North Pole in 1932, probably having hibernated in Tolkien's imagination since he read Macdonald's *Princess and the Goblin* as a child. "Goblins are to us very much what rats are to you, only worse, because they are very clever" (1932). Their worst enemies are Gnomes. As World War II drew nearer and nearer, Father Christmas mentioned Goblins "breeding again and multiplying all over the world" (1935). He also says there was trouble with them in 1453. Why then? Tolkien when being so precise must have something precise in mind. The martyrdom of Joan of Arc was too early, the Wars of the Roses just too late. What went on at the North Pole in 1453 is not documented; but in that year England was defeated at the Battle of Castillon, where the French made notable use of cannon. That ended the Hundred Years' War and the English occupation of France except for Calais. But the English power in France had been diminishing since 1429; and Tolkien, who had fought in France himself, would be more likely to agree with Joan of Arc that "God does love Englishmen—in England" than to mourn Castillon. His mind was more probably at the other end of Christendom, where in 1453 Constantinople fell to the Turks in an assault involving both bombs and treachery: nothing could be more characteristic of goblins as shown in Tolkien's later works.[9]

Father Christmas alludes to his Green Brother (1930), who is probably the spirit of the summer solstice as Father Christmas is of the winter one.[10] That is, Father Christmas is the son of Grandfather Yule, a personification of the solstice as happy cosmic event: now our days get longer. In the present age we associate the season with the birth of Christ, to mingle mankind's current happiness with age-old hemispheric good news.

The Father Christmas letters show some of Tolkien's perennial interests: feasting and gift-giving, alphabets, goblins, caves. Some of the artwork is at least as distinguished as the writing: the glass window in 1929, the reindeer in 1938, the sleigh over Oxford shown with the introduction, and the parody of cave drawings in 1932 (with several styles), are strikingly deft. But I should venture to say that a great many loving and imaginative parents in the world could do as well. With all the letters' charm, they hold a minor place in the corpus of Tolkien's subcreation.

Not so *The Hobbit*. Though the book is a juvenile and as different from *The Silmarillion* and *The Lord of the Rings* as they from each other, its importance equals theirs. One summer in the late 1920s, as Tolkien was marking School Certificate exams—he did so every year for the money—he came upon a blank page, "(which is the best thing that can possibly happen to an examiner) and I wrote on it: '*In a hole in the ground there lived a hobbit.*' Names always generate a story in my mind. Eventually I thought I'd better find out what hobbits were like."[11]

Carpenter stresses Tolkien's attitude of the explorer rather than the inventor: he *finds out* what his new words and strange references mean, as if his material had "a real extra-mental existence."[12] Clearly this attitude of his, along with his skill and enormous knowledge, contributes to the conviction which his stories carry to many of their readers. His entire work could be ranged under the heading of Father Christmas's words about one of his pictures: "imaginary, but more or less as it really is" (*FCL*, intro.).

Hobbits, Tolkien "found out," share the smug, ordered provincialism of Sinclair Lewis's Babbitt (1922):

They are (or were) small people. . . . There is little or no magic about them. . . . They are inclined to be fat in the stomach; they dress in bright colours (chiefly green and yellow); wear no shoes, because their feet grow natural leathery soles and thick warm brown hair like the stuff on their heads. . .; have long, clever brown fingers, good-natured faces, and laugh deep fruity laughs (especially after dinner, which they have twice a day when they can get it).[14]

They resemble the people of Sarehole: "rustic English people, made small in size because it reflects the generally small reach of their imagination."[15] Indeed, Tolkien says,

I am in fact a hobbit (in all but size). I like gardens, trees and un-mechanized farmlands; I smoke a pipe, and like good plain food (un-refrigerated), but detest French cooking; I like, and even dare to wear in these dull days [1958], ornamental waistcoats. I am fond of mushrooms (out of a field); have a very simple sense of humor (which even my appreciative critics find tiresome); I go to bed late and get up late (when possible). I do not travel much. (Letter, appendix).

Given that hobbits are such creatures, it seems that writing a story about them would indeed be chronicling small beer; "days that are good to spend are . . . not much to listen to" (*H*, 60). How is the writer to get hobbits into a plot? "We are plain quiet folk and have no use for adventures. Nasty disturbing uncomfortable things! Make you late for dinner!" (*H*, 18).

To one particular hobbit at his hole comes a figure from a German postcard Tolkien had: a bearded man in a broad-brimmed hat, with Alps in the background. On the green rounded hill of the Shire appears the Mountain Spirit, become the wizard Gandalf.[16] Now Tolkien's hobbit hero, Bilbo Baggins, can be involved willy-nilly. Token and the wizard will send him "There and Back Again" on that fool-proof plot, the Quest.

What is a quest for? Treasure, of course. Whose treasure? Tolkien's beloved Norse mythology makes clear that the best and most powerful treasures are made by dwarves, and that treasures are hoarded by dragons. A set of dwarves and a hobbit against a dragon: there's a plot. Dwarves may think they have no need of a hobbit—"He looks more like a grocer than a burglar" (*H*, 30)—but *there is more to Bilbo than meets the eye*. Tolkien continued his remark about the small reach of hobbits' imaginations with "not the small reach of their courage or latent power."[17] Hobbits shall show what Tolkien most admires in humankind: the final dauntlessness of those who seem, even to themselves, petty.

The Eddas supply Tolkien with a handful of authentic dwarf names,[18] and the story is under way: Thorin and Company are off to Erebor the Lonely Mountain, to recover, with Bilbo's help, their ancestral treasure from Smaug. Tolkien spun the tale for John, Michael, and Christopher "in our Winter 'Reads' after tea in the evening."[19]

Bilbo and the rest move through well-thought-out landscapes and ever-growing perils. Tolkien had made a map of *The Hobbit*'s territory almost as soon as he conceived the story; he imagined places as urgently as narratives. Norse folklore furnished trolls as the first antagonists. The speech of the three trolls in *The Hobbit* was doubtless furnished by disgruntled Tommies overheard by Lieutenant Tolkien: "Mutton yesterday, mutton today, and blimey, if it don't look like mutton again tomorrer" (*H*, 46). Bilbo tries a bit of burgling and gets caught, with all the dwarves after him. Gandalf rescues them, exploiting the well-documented effect of actinic radiation on troll metabolism: sunlight turns them to stone. The companions then make free of the trolls' food and treasure; Bilbo gets a dagger which makes a small sword for him.

The travelers have a respite at the Last Homely House West of the Mountains, where they and Tolkien's readers first meet elves. A frivolous lot they look, teasing the dwarves and the hobbit: "Don't dip your beard in the foam, father! It is long enough without watering it." "Mind Bilbo doesn't eat all the cakes. He is too fat to get through keyholes yet!" (*H*, 60). Gandalf counsels them to discretion. We learn that elves are actually the reverse of foolish, and that Bilbo loves them but dwarves do not. Tolkien introduces Elrond, chief of the "people who had both elves and heroes of the North for ancestors" (*H*, 60).

The matter of cross-fertile races is treated at more length in chapter 5. It is not stressed in *The Hobbit*. The original version of the story lightly remarks that because of the exotic doings of the Took family, other hobbits say "that long ago one or other of the Tooks had married into a fairy family (the less friendly said a goblin family)" (*H*, 16). The more Tolkien wrote of his history, the more plainly impossible this allegation became, even as a rumor; so the third edition of *The Hobbit* (1966) attenuates it to "It was often said (in other families) that long ago one of the Took ancestors must have taken a fairy wife. That was, of course, absurd. . . ."

After leaving Elrond and Rivendell, the company traverses the Misty Mountains. There live stone-giants, mentioned briefly in *The Hobbit* and not at all in *The Lord of the Rings*. Since the rest of Tolkien's work has no giants as such, one may speculate that these stone-giants are some kind of troll; brief remarks in *The Lord of the Rings* indicate that there are several kinds of trolls, and Tolkien gives us few details of any. Gandalf's reference to the possibility of finding a "more or less decent giant" (*H*, 99) may or may not rule out trolls; a reader's conclusion will depend on whether he takes "Perry-the-Winkle" (*ATB*, 4) as pure fantasy.

Sheltering in a cave, the travelers are captured by goblins. Not the small vermin which trouble the North Pole, but more-than-dwarf-sized creatures, hostile to the world in general and Thorin's kin in particular. Gandalf, with his characteristic fire-craft, routs the goblins, frees the dwarves, and leads them under the mountains and out the other side.

But Bilbo gets dropped, knocked out, and lost in the tunnels. Crawling alone in the dark, he feels a metal ring on the floor and pockets it.

The chapter "Riddles in the Dark" was revised by Tolkien in 1951 for the second edition of *The Hobbit*; his work on the further history of the Third Age had shown that the version he had told his children and published in 1937 could not be completely true. Therefore, says Tolkien—as editor of the Red Book of Westmarch, the hobbits' own history[20]—Bilbo must have biased the story, which means something sinister was befalling his honest hobbit character.

Both versions agree that Bilbo found the ring (the Ring, as it later turned out to be), met Gollum, engaged in the riddle-game, and with Gollum's guidance found his way out of the mountains, escaping the goblin guards because the ring made him invisible. The first and second editions differ in the precise coloring of the characters, the second showing both as grimmer and the situation as more fearful. Tolkien's revisions also point to some sort of will in the ring.[21]

We do not learn from either version that Gollum is a degenerated proto-hobbit. He is old, dark—but for his luminescent eyes—small and slimy (the second edition adds). He has a nervous habit of gulping, hence the nickname of Gollum. He eats goblins, which cannot raise him in the reader's estimation no matter how antigoblin one feels; and he is quite prepared to eat Bilbo.

But Bilbo has his dagger from the troll-hoard, which has turned out to be an ancient blade from the goblin wars of Gondolin. The presence of the sword is all the explanation given at the time for Gollum's becoming "quite polite." Unlike any other antagonist—troll, goblin, spider, or even wood-elf—Gollum starts a conversation: "Praps ye sits here and chats with it a bitsy, my preciousss" (*H*, 80). During the riddle-game, we are given glimpses of an earlier life of Gollum's, living in sunlight on a riverbank with kin, "when he had been less lonely and sneaky and nasty" (*H*, 82). One need not stress these details in reading *The Hobbit*, but even in the first edition, Tolkien's foundation is laid for the role Gollum plays in *The Lord of the Rings*.

The riddle-contest is another Norse feature: a prominent event in *The Saga of King Heidrek the Wise*, which Christopher Tolkien grew up to edit.[22] A character who is Odin in disguise ends the contest by asking what Odin said in a certain private conversation: not a riddle, but the question defeats his opponent. So with Bilbo: searching for another riddle, he pats his clothes and mutters, "What have I got in my pocket?" Gollum takes it for a riddle, though not a fair one, and they agree on three guesses. Gollum cannot guess the ring.

His forfeit differs in the two versions. In the first, Bilbo's doctored story, Gollum had pledged a "present," meaning the ring. Unable to find it, he agreed to show Bilbo out instead. Thus Bilbo had not only found the ring but also won it.

In the corrected version, the end of the Gollum chapter is far more frightening. Bilbo's prize was to be that Gollum showed him out. But Gollum, warped, sore, and hungry, went to get the ring, become invisible, and attack Bilbo. Finding it missing, he guesses what was in Bilbo's pocket and rushes back in a murderous rage. But Gollum's frantic monologue has alerted Bilbo to some of the ring's value, and it slips onto his finger (so phrased, implying the ring is an agent) so that Gollum misses him. Then Gollum heads for the exit, followed by Bilbo invisible. As the bereaved creature crouches in the mouth of the last tunnel, Bilbo leaps over him and escapes out the goblin-guarded door. After him echoes Gollum's wail, "Thief, thief, thief! Baggins! We hates it, we hates it, we hates it for ever!"

Both versions of the episode show Bilbo braver and more resourceful than he or we had any occasion to expect. Even in the true version his conduct is not to be condemned—odd that his conscience should prick him to doctor the story. Though acting in a nasty predicament to save his life, he must have felt touched on the raw by Gollum's epithet "tricksy." The implication is that his feelings toward the ring were such that he *would have* committed trickery to keep it. Not fully conscious of that, he still felt an obscure unease, which Gandalf suspected in listening to Bilbo's version of his escape. More important than Bilbo's unease, or his shrewdness (alias trickiness), or even his newfound courage, was a fourth quality he showed with Gollum. As the disgusting creature crouched ready to spring, blocking the tunnel to escape, the invisible hobbit could have killed him. Instead, Bilbo felt pity and acted with mercy. One could say that there, by nonviolence, under the mountains in a children's book, the War of the Ring was won.[23]

If the true version of the episode shows Bilbo as marginally "tricksy," it shows Gollum much worse: as soon as he lost the "sacred" riddle-game, he planned to attack Bilbo. In the first version, Gollum could be perceived as almost comic, with his "Bless us and splash us, my precioussss!" (*H,* 79). The second version shows the depth of his misery and wickedness. He has survived far longer than his kind's life span—it transpires in *The Lord of the Rings*—and passed nearly five hundred years in isolation under the mountains, with nothing but the precious ring, which devours his mind.[24] The revised *Hobbit* begins to show Gollum's dual nature. In the first edition, he calls himself "we"; in the second, he holds a whole conversation with himself. A reader of *The Hobbit* might think of this only as convenient exposition, to tell the listening Bilbo about the ring; but it foreshadows Gollum's split personality revealed in *The Lord of the Rings*, where both personalities play vital roles.

Gollum, like Bilbo, is Tolkien's own creature, borrowed from no skald or romantic.[25] The way Tolkien fits his original subcreations together with his various borrowings, with no obtrusive seams, is one feature of his skill.

Outside the mountains, Bilbo reluctantly decides he must go back and look for the dwarves and Gandalf. How different from the hobbit who overslept as the expedition first left Hobbiton! Just then he finds them safe, and raises his stock by sneaking past Balin on lookout duty. Rather than being miffed, the dwarf becomes his particular friend. Bilbo keeps the ring secret and receives a queer look from Gandalf.

Invisible rings are no help when the company is treed by wolves, wargs who cooperate with the goblins. "Escaping goblins to be caught by wolves!" (*H,* 103), cries Bilbo, and Tolkien tells us the words became a proverb. He often coins proverbs for his secondary world, which add to our impression of its solidity.[26] Gandalf's fires hold the wolves off, but the goblins who come out at nightfall (sunlight makes them sick) use the fire against the trees where the company have taken refuge. They are rescued by eagles, a regal and solitary race whose lord Gandalf once healed of an arrow wound. Since human beings shoot them—another slap at our race's destructiveness—the eagles carry the travelers to a spot far from the woodmen's settlements.

Their next host is a great gruff man named Beorn. A man by day, but by night a bear: what the Québecois call a wendigo, a were-bear. This is another "low philological jest"[27] on Tolkien's part, depending on the likeness of the Norse words *beorn* ("warrior") and *bjorn* ("bear").

Tolkien, like other scholars of sagas, has puzzled about berserkers. They rush into battle in a special rage (*berserkergang*); they chew their shields; weapons do not bite on them. Questions abound: did people really think they turned into bears?[28] Even if human beings do not turn into bears, the word berserk raises questions. A sark is a shirt: did they wear bearskin shirts? If so, was it to turn weapons, to invoke the strength of bears, or to frighten the enemy? Or did they strip in their battle-rage and rush forth *bare*-sark? The story of weapons not biting on them is not surprising; ordinary people engaging in intense physical activity notice pain markedly less. "I wonder where I got that bruise?"[29]

Beorn is a shape-changer "under no enchantment but his own" (*H*, 118). It may seem remarkable that all his sheep, horses, and dogs would work for a part-time bear; but the abundance of bees and flowers testifies to the preferred diet of the bear as well as the man. His fierceness is all on the moral plane: the bear's victims are goblins and wargs. Goblins may have dispossessed him and his from the mountains (*H*, 118–19).

The dwarves keep appearing at his house the way they did at Bilbo's hole. Beorn lends them ponies to replace those the goblins ate.[30] Supplied by him, they ride to the eaves of Mirkwood (Norse, "border-wood," rather than murky). At this point, Gandalf leaves the dwarves and Bilbo, adding his warning to Beorn's that they must not leave the path.

Mirkwood is as full of dread as the Wild Wood in *The Wind in the Willows*. Bombur, the fattest dwarf, falls into an enchanted stream which puts him to sleep, and having to carry him depresses the group's morale still further. They hear a mysterious hunt and see white deer,[31] but no people. When Bombur wakes, he keeps talking about his dream of food, lights, and merrymakers in the woods; so when the famished group sees lights off to one side, they leave the path. One breaks fairy-tale prohibitions at one's peril.

They find an elf-ring, like a larger edition of the dinner Gildor treats the hobbits to in *The Fellowship of the Ring* (chapter 3). But out go the lights at the dwarves' appearance, and the company loses each other in the dark, until the dwarves' voices fade away and Bilbo is again left alone.

He wakes in the toils of a giant spider. Tolkien had been bitten by a tarantula in South Africa, and Michael had a horror of spiders, as do many people; so the author could be drawing on either personal or public feeling in his portrayal of arachnids.[32] Bilbo slashes himself free and kills his attacker. "Somehow the killing of the giant spider, all alone by himself in the dark without the help of the wizard or the dwarves or of anyone else, made a great difference to Mr. Baggins. He felt a different person, and much fiercer and bolder in spite of an empty stomach" (*H*, 154). He christens his sword Sting and sets out to search for the dwarves. They too are captured by spiders. Bilbo uses the ring, his accurate throwing-arm, Sting, and all his wit and courage in rescuing them. Once safe—from spiders, at least—in an elf-ring, he explains about his ring of invisibility. The dwarves have come to look on him as a leader.

Thorin is missing, captured by Wood-elves. Tolkien takes the occasion to sketch some elven history: some groups spent generations in "Faerie in the West," but Wood-elves and some others stayed in the Wide World (Middle-earth) "before the raising [*sic*] of the Sun and Moon" (*H*, 164). *The Silmarillion*, on which Tolkien had been working for some twenty years when *The Hobbit* came out, gives an exact account: the Wood-elves are Avari, Moriquendi, "dark elves," because they never beheld the light of the two trees of Valinor.

Tolkien is drawing on Norse mythology again, which uses the terms *ljossalfar* and *döckalfar*, though the lore of light and dark elves is scattered, unsystematic, and contradictory. Tolkien remedies this in his mythic history. The passage on elves (*H*, 164–65) got revised in the third edition. Tolkien drops the term "gnomes" for Deep-elves (the Noldor), and adds that the Avari "loved best the stars."[33] Thorin's captors are "more dangerous and less wise" than the Calaquendi; "Still elves they were and remain, and that is Good People" (*H*, 164–65). Their king is named in *The Lord of the Rings* as Thranduil.

We hear of a long-standing animosity between these particular elves and the dwarves: had the latter stolen elf-treasure, or simply kept a fee for shaping the metals and jewels? Tolkien does not commit himself. Thorin will tell Thranduil no word of their quest, so he is imprisoned; also fed. The rest of the dwarves are captured and Bilbo, invisible, tags along. He skulks for weeks in the elves' cave-palace.

Longing as usual for his hobbit-hole—this forms a refrain throughout the book—Bilbo "soon realized that if anything was to be done, it would have to be done by Mr. Baggins alone and unaided" (*H*, 170). Though he "did not like being depended on by everyone" (*H*, 171), he engineered their escape, floated down-river in barrels.

Thus Bilbo and the dwarves reach Esgaroth, Lake-town, built on piles. Its people—human beings—acclaim Thorin as the returned King under the Mountain. Duly cosseted and re-provisioned, the party sets out for the Lonely Mountain. "They were come to the Desolation of the Dragon, and they were come at the waning of the year" (*H*, 195): brief as this sentence is, it exemplifies Tolkien's ability to evoke the mood of a place and season.

A map of Thorin's shows an entrance to the mountain besides Smaug's gate; and moon-letters discovered by Elrond give mysterious instructions: "Stand by the grey stone when the thrush knocks, and the setting sun with the last light of Durin's Day will shine upon the key-hole" (*H*, 62). They find a rock wall which must be the door, and in a manner parallel to the scene at the gates of Moria in *The Fellowship of the Ring*, try vainly to open it. Finally Bilbo recognizes the moment described by the moon-runes. The door is open, their way is clear—to the dragon's lair.

What does a burglar do with a dragon's hoard? *Beowulf* has told Tolkien that: he takes a cup. So Bilbo does. Approaching the rumbling cave "was the bravest thing he ever did" (*H*, 205). He beholds the great sleeping dragon and the dwarves' hoard. Even Bilbo is roused to lust for the vast treasure: an emotion Tolkien particularly fears, though events prove Bilbo's fit was but momentary.

As the dwarves admire the cup, Smaug wakes to "the sort of

rage that is only seen when rich folk that have more than they can enjoy suddenly lose something that they have long had but never before used or wanted" (*H*, 208). He scorches the mountainside; Bilbo and Thorin get the dwarves into the tunnel just in time.

In their predicament, the hobbit takes the lead, volunteering to go down invisible and scout again. "Had he known more about dragons and their wily ways, he might have been more frightened and less hopeful" (*H*, 211). Still, Bilbo comes off fairly well in the ensuing conversation with Smaug. He had unwarily given his name to Gollum, but properly answers Smaug's questions with riddling phrases. Tolkien has learned from Norse lore and passes on to us "the way to talk to dragons" (*H*, 213).

Smaug does his best to sow mistrust between Bilbo and the dwarves. Though he makes the hobbit most uncomfortable, their conversation is only a shadow of the tragic confrontation of Glaurung and Turin in *The Silmarillion*; *The Hobbit* is after all a juvenile. Bilbo's mention of revenge sends Smaug into a gab or boasting speech of psalmlike intensity:

Revenge! The King under the Mountain is dead and where are his kin that dare seek revenge? Girion Lord of Dale is dead, and I have eaten his people like a wolf among sheep, and where are his sons' sons that dare approach me? I kill where I wish and none dare resist. I laid low the warriors of old and their like is not in the world today. Then I was but young and tender. Now I am old and strong, strong, strong. Thief in the shadows! My armour is like tenfold shields, my teeth are swords, my claws spears, the shock of my tail a thunderbolt, my wings a hurricane, and my breath death! (*H*, 215–16)

Using flattery, Bilbo discovers a vital nugget of information: the dragon's gem-studded belly has a bare spot.

Bilbo reports this to the dwarves, overheard by the thrush who was knocking when the keyhole appeared. The men of Dale used to talk with the thrushes. Reminiscing about the hoard, Thorin recalls the Arkenstone (Anglo-Saxon, "precious stone"), in a very Tolkienian description: "It was like a globe with a thousand facets; it shone like silver in the firelight, like water in the sun, like snow under the stars, like rain upon the Moon!" (*H*, 220).

Bilbo, for no discernable reason, urges the dwarves to enter the tunnel and shut the door. At that moment, Smaug devastates the entire west side of the mountain. Apparently the hobbit has not only courage and wit, but sometimes intuition or ESP. He has, in fact, the intangible but often-believed-in *luck* which accompanies heroes until their deaths: the luck which the Norsemen believed made a leader worth following (e.g., Leif the Lucky).

Smaug, convinced that the group came from Esgaroth, flies off to destroy the wooden town. Bard, a grim warrior of the line of Dale, recognizes the approaching "air-raid" and gets some defense set up. As the town nevertheless flames to ruin, the thrush comes to tell Bard where to place his last arrow. "With a shriek that deafened men, felled trees and split stone,"[34] the dragon dies. The survivors of Lake-town are helped by some of the host of Thranduil, who has set out for the unguarded treasure. Warriors of Esgaroth join the elves who head for the Mountain.

Meanwhile the dwarves, though expecting Smaug's return, have set up camp and reacquainted themselves with the hoard. Bilbo the burglar, sent ahead as usual, has found and pocketed the Arkenstone. "They did say I could pick and choose my own share; and I think I would choose this, if they took all the rest!" (*H*, 226). Told of the dragon's death and the mustering of hosts, Thorin takes the position that not a carat of gold leaves the mountain, and the thirteen dwarves and Bilbo dig in for a siege.

Bard asks for a parley, but Thorin remains adamant: "While an armed host lies before our doors, we look on you as foes and thieves" (*H*, 251). When he goes so far as to fire upon a herald, the siege is declared.

Here, fully fleshed even in a juvenile, is the Tolkienian question again: Who is a hero? What does a hero do? Thorin, posted immovably on his ancestral treasure, has taken a heroic stance—and the author openly declares him wrong. Bard, warrior and dragon-slayer, obviously *is* a hero. Does he want to fight? No, he wants to parley; but his will is frustrated. The master of Lake-town, his mind on comfort and prosperity, is clearly a worm and no man. Bilbo Baggins is self-evidently not a hero, yet he is *the* hero of this book. What does a hero do?

Burglar Baggins sneaks out by night, before the army of Thorin's kin can arrive, and meets Bard and Thranduil. Pointing out the awkwardness of the situation for all concerned, Bilbo says he has something "to aid you in your bargaining." And "not without a shudder, not without a glance of longing" (*H*, 257), he gives them the breathtaking Arkenstone. He sets aside his personal desire, in order to win peace for all. Then he insists on returning to his companions. A cloaked figure rises and cries, "Well done!" (*H*, 258). Gandalf has reappeared.

Not only does Bilbo go back to the dwarves, but the next day when Thorin asks how the men and elves came by the stone, the hobbit squeaks, "I gave it them!" (*H*, 261). The question of what a hero does is answered, no matter how unheroic the manner of his actions.

Dwarf reinforcements arrive, and are on the point of joining battle with the men and elves when a common enemy transforms the fight: goblins swarm with their wolves and bats to Erebor. Tolkien's description of the battle is breathlessly concise and clear. His sense of terrain in adventure equals John Buchan's. The advantage swings back and forth. As elves, dwarves, and men are about to sink in defeat, the eagles arrive (*aquila ex machina*). They had marked the goblin muster and now turn the tide. Beorn appears as a bear—no weapon hurts him—to crush the goblin chief. But Thorin is wounded mortally. His last act is to make up with Bilbo: "If more of us valued food and cheer and song above hoarded gold, it would be a merrier world" (*H*, 273).

Tolkien carefully ties up loose ends. All characters are dealt with justly and seen home. Bilbo's return is jarred by his stumbling into his own estate sale, featuring his acquisitive cousins the Sackville-Bagginses. As he settles again in the Shire, he finds himself "no longer quite respectable" (*H*, 285). But as a friend of elves, dwarves, and his own young cousins, he "remained very happy to the end of his days, and those were extraordinarily long" (*H*, 285). The book closes as it opened, with a call from Gandalf. Bilbo, brought up to date on news from the East, exclaims,

"Then the prophecies of the old song have turned out to be true, after a fashion!"

"Of course!" said Gandalf. . . . "Surely you don't disbelieve the prophecies because you had a hand in bringing them about yourself? You don't really suppose, do you, that all your adventures and escapes were managed by mere luck, just for your sole benefit? You are a very fine person, Mr. Baggins, and I am very fond of you; but you are only quite a little fellow in a wide world, after all!"

"Thank goodness!" said Bilbo laughing, and handed him the tobacco-jar. (*H*, 286–87)

The Hobbit was soon recognized as an outstanding children's book. The writer has dealt—in detail and without preaching—with the theme of a person's maturing, a matter of unending import to readers. Not only that, but the secondary world of his book—characters, places, and objects—gives an impression of unusual depth and solidity. Readers of *The Hobbit* in 1937 did not know that Tolkien had been working for some twenty years on a mythology, and his children's story had hooks to that world. And not only in theme and setting but in language, the philological professor was presenting caviar to the public— which it did appreciate. His usage is supple, fitting each of his varied situations: from himself explaining to his sons what a hobbit is;[35] through the understated modern English speech of hobbits, Beorn's homeliness, and the old-fashioned formality of the parleys before Erebor; to the poetic descriptions of the Arkenstone. And the book is studded with verses: all Tolkien's races, even goblins, have their proper songs.[36] His names are flawless—rare for even excellent fantasy writers.[37] Tolkien, in fact, revels in his words as much as any dragon in his hoard; but his audience of live children insured his *sharing* of the treasure.

His efforts were appreciated. Michael, joining the service in World War II and tired of filling out forms, answered "Father's Occupation" with "wizard."[38]

CHAPTER 5

Mythic History

G ENESIS and geology set Tolkien to pondering. Either can fascinate, and both in one mind can generate remarkable results.[1] Unlike Sherlock Holmes, Tolkien cared to know that he lived on a globular body orbiting its sun in a period of three hundred and sixty-five days, five hours, forty-eight minutes, and forty-six seconds.[2] From his care for this world and its people grew his longest-nurtured book, *The Silmarillion*: an account of our planet, though it may "look like nothing on Earth."

Tolkien enjoyed natural history as a child, and evidently had a fair layman's knowledge of geology: he correctly equates beryl with emerald (I, 269, 308), and Father Christmas refers to a "time, long ago, when the North Pole was somewhere else" (1932). Wegener's book on continental drift was published in an English translation in 1924; and either it or ideas from it reached Tolkien, as his secondary world indicates. Landmasses have been torn asunder, and Tolkien as mythographer shows why. People with training in various sciences of the primary world have been repeatedly impressed with the believability of Tolkien's out-and-out fantasy.[3]

It is not recorded whether any teacher at King Edward's School ever demonstrated time to the boys by unrolling a strip of paper all round the room, making a pin scratch across the end, and saying, "That is the amount of time covered by the history we know"; but again, such knowledge entered Tolkien's mind: there have been eons unknown to us. As he supplied the Gothic lexicon with words he needed, using known laws of word formation, he decided to fill in past time with events, applying what he knew of history formation.

He would use what written sources he could find. A document purporting to cover time from its beginning would be of interest:

hence Genesis. Tolkien's relation to the Bible was of a median sort: as a Catholic, he knew the Bible was true, inspired, the book of God's stories for this age of the world. But as a Catholic again, he was not a fundamentalist: did not believe every word of the Bible to be literally true, even in the languages of its origin, let alone in all the translations to which his linguistic studies gave him access. He himself was marginally involved with the English translation of the Jerusalem Bible (published in 1966), working on the Book of Jonah.[4]

The thirteenth-century Dominican Thomas Aquinas had set forth with his characteristic clarity the various ways besides the literal in which biblical texts can be interpreted. Human beings can express themselves in words; but God (Thomas reasons) can express Himself with both words and the things the words refer to. Objects and events, not only the stories of them, are messages to our race from God.[5]

Though not a fundamentalist, Tolkien in his mythology uses mostly the historical or literal sense of the Bible, leaving aside Thomas's allegorical, tropological, and anagogical senses. As a believer, Tolkien does not go head-to-head with the Bible on any point. The origin of the human race and the coming of evil to that race (original sin), for instance, are perfectly well covered in Genesis. But on matters which the Bible leaves vague, Tolkien's mythopoeic urge cried for light in the void. The chief of these matters in his mind were three: the heavenly bodies, the disaster by water, and the races. The image of "Earendel, brightest of angels"[6] settled in his mind with certain other pieces of mythology; it is time to examine those pieces.

Genesis begins at the beginning of our universe, with the creation of light. Students of our planet have found that the biblical order of creation—plants, sea animals, land animals, man—conforms to the evidence they can find, with one great anomaly: according to Genesis, light was created on the first day, plants on the third, but the sun and moon not until the fourth. Since the light we know is localized in the sun, and plants need it, Genesis is puzzling. Tolkien could not conclude that the Bible was untrue, but he could certainly conclude that further explanation was needed. He was a skeptic in the proper

sense of the word (Greek *skepsis,* "looking"): one who examines
his beliefs, not an unbeliever.

At some periods, stars have been believed to rule human
destinies.[7] The Old Testament undercuts belief in astrology
by consistently referring to the stars as creatures of God, never
themselves rulers. In some biblical poetry they are personified:
God reminds Job of his human ignorance of the time of
creation, "When the morning stars praised me together, and
all the sons of God made a joyful melody."[8]

The tale of the disaster by water is not scanted in Genesis:
Noah's flood receives full treatment in chapters 6–8. So why
does Tolkien, who generally devotes his energy to writing
around the Bible, make the story of Numenor and its sinking
so important? The answer is not only the world's mythology
(every land has a flood story), but—personal experience. As a
dream gave Tolkien "Leaf by Niggle," dreams connected him
with the fall of Numenor. As a child he dreamed "of the in-
eluctable Wave, either coming up out of a quiet sea, or coming
in towering over the green inlands."[9] Something in Tolkien
insisted on hearing more than the Bible told of the disaster by
water. Where Genesis has a huge temporary flood, he has one
land sunk forever. He came to refer to the dream as his
"Atlantis-haunting."[10]

Atlantis, the skeletal story and an expanded account, is found
first in the dialogues of Plato. No documents survive to tell
how far he was repeating current beliefs and how much
inventing to make a point. In *Timaeus,* the greatest exploit of
prehistoric Athenians was to defeat the empire-seeking forces
of a powerful "island situated in front of ... the pillars of
Heracles; it was larger than Lybia and Asia put together, and
was the way to other islands, and from these you might pass
to the whole of the opposite continent which surrounded the
true ocean." But after Athens had defeated Atlantis, "there
occurred violent earthquakes and floods; and in a single day
and night of misfortune ... the island of Atlantis ... disap-
peared in the depths of the sea."[11] In *Critias,* Plato spreads
himself on a description of the island; but the dialogue breaks
off just as he is saying that the kings' divine blood got diluted,
and while still looking glorious, they fell into degeneracy. So

the gods decided. . . . This outline can provide grist for tendentious works or thrillers and has done so to this day.[12] In Tolkien's stories, though the place of Numenor is pivotal—its downfall determines the present shape of our earth—the writer spends less time on Numenor itself than on the ages before and after it.

As important to Tolkien as it is enigmatic in Genesis is the matter of the races. Here is the account from the beginning of the sixth chapter: "When human beings became numerous on the face of the Earth, and daughters were born to them, the *Bene Elohim* saw that the human daughters were beautiful, and took any they chose for wives. . . . The *Nephilim* were on Earth in those days and afterward, when the *Bene Elohim* were mating and having children with the daughters of men; those were the heroes, famous men of old." This passage, especially the words left untranslated, must evoke speculation. *Someone* was cross-fertile with human beings; and *someone* inhabited this planet then but by implication not now. Even the words which are clear have ambiguities in their syntax: are the Nephilim, the offspring of Bene Elohim and humans, and the heroes all the same, or if not, which does "heroes" mean?

The words "Bene Elohim" mean "Sons of the High," and the phrase is usually translated "Sons of God." It could mean that godly human beings, descendants of Seth, married worse-disposed human beings, descendants of Cain; or that sons of rulers married daughters of commoners. But Hebrew uses "son of" to mean "member of the species of." That sense could imply some race of lowercase gods on the chain of being between humankind and the Creator: beings enough like man to marry and beget children. The Bible says no more about them, but the polytheistic religions surrounding the Jews were full of such creatures. Begetting heroes on beautiful human beings was a specialty with the Greek Zeus, for instance.

The Hebrew word *Nephilim* is not clear; its meaning is nebulous. It suggests "those who have gone down," or "the miscarried." It has usually been translated as "giants."[13] It appears that starting with the *Nephilim*, Tolkien caught the ball and ran in three directions. During his Anglo-Saxon studies, reading Aelfric's translation of Genesis, Tolkien found that

"Entas wearon . . . ofer eorthan on tham dagum." *Ent*, an Anglo-Saxon word for giant, was taken by Tolkien for the name of his fourteen-foot-tall tree-people, tallest of his races.

But *Nephilim* carries other ideas. Hebrew is no Indo-European language; but unrelated words can sound alike. Indo-European has a root *nebh*, meaning something to do with cloud. It appears in the Greek *nephos* ("cloud"), which certainly sounds like Nephilim. And *Farmer Giles* shows that for Tolkien's stories, a sound-suggestion is all he needs. *Nephilim* sounds like "cloud-people" and quite possibly stands behind Tolkien's description of the Valar appearing in *fanar*, an Elvish word whose primary meaning was "veil" or "cloud." The word

was applied to the "veils" or "raiment" in which the *Valar* presented themselves to physical eyes. These were the bodies in which they were self-incarnated. They usually took the shape of the bodies of Elves (and Men). The *Valar* assumed these forms . . . because of their love and desire for the Children of God (*Erusén*). . . . The future forms of Elves and Men had been revealed to them. . . . In these *Fanar* they . . . appeared as persons of majestic (but not gigantic) stature, vested in robes expressing their individual natures and functions. . . . these forms were always in some degree radiant, as if suffused with a light from within . . . , (*RGEO*, 66)

like a cloud with the sun behind it. This passage also shows Tolkien's interpretation of "Sons of God," enlarged upon in *The Silmarillion*.

Tolkien knew not only Greek, but Germanic mythology; and to a lover of that lore, Genesis sounds arrestingly as if it said, "the Nibelungen were on Earth in those days." Who are Nibelungen? Unfortunately for clarity but perhaps fortunately for imagination, Germanic sources use the word in different ways. The most conspicuous medieval use of the term is in the title of the *Nibelungenlied*, a German poem of around 1200 which seems to reflect some events of the fifth century. In it, Nibelungs are human beings: first those from whom Siegfried wins a certain treasure and afterward his family-in-law, the Burgundians. The term shifts with possession of the treasure. "Through Siegfried the Frankish Welisungs [Volsungs] get linked to the Burgundian Gibichungs, and then both are called Nibelungs."[14]

Etymologically, Nibelungs are not human beings (natives of Middle-earth); they are natives of Niflheim, the cold and misty (*nebh*) ninth world. Yet Niflheim is said to be inhabited by *svartalfar*, black elves, different from the *döckalfar* whom Tolkien has accounted for with his Moriquendi. Grimm finds evidence that *svartalfar* are dwarves; and Wagner in his Ring operas makes the Nibelungen dwarvish miners and smiths. So it seems likely that Tolkien's third response to the word *Nephilim*, besides the Ents and the cloudlike *fanar*, was the name of his petty-dwarves: Noegyth *Nibin*.

Student of the world's stories, galled by unexplained bits of mythology, Tolkien reacted like an oyster to an irritant and built pearls round them.

He did not start his mythology at the beginning and write straight through, but would compose a story he wanted—sometimes in verse and prose both—and then find out how it hooked onto other matters. Because of his knowing and marrying Edith, the story of Beren and Luthien came early in his work. So did the defeat of the Hidden City; for in the 1920s, when the undergraduate Neville Coghill asked Tolkien to read a paper to a club, the professor agreed: he would read "Forragonglin." Coghill tried to act as if he understood, and the club was presented with "The Fall of Gondolin," which now stands two thirds of the way through *The Silmarillion*.

Allen and Unwin's reader, confronted with a pile of Tolkien's mythology, spoke of "eye-splitting Celtic names." Tolkien said, "Needless to say they are not Celtic!"[15] The names seem more overwhelming in *The Silmarillion* than in Tolkien's other stories because there is less narrative padding round them, less leisure in which to know the bearers of the names. Tolkien's style, in this book especially, is at the opposite pole from modern psychologizing novels, which analyze their characters' processes at discursive length.[16] Tolkien will only give a short, pregnant line: "Celegorm and Curufin said nothing, but they smiled and went from the halls."[17] His brevity gives the reader as much unease as a page on Celegorm and Curufin's ulterior motives.

The book as we have it contains not only "The History of the Silmarils" proper, but also four shorter sections bridging back to creation and forward to the War of the Ring.

Creation begins with the Ainur. The Bible, steadfastly and

polemically monotheistic, deals with humankind and the Creator, slighting other beings; nevertheless their existence shows round the edges.[18] They are called "spirits," a word which meant "breath" but was used to express "that which is of nature different from matter/energy." There is a well-established tradition that before the creation of the matter/energy universe, God made personal beings of spirit, and that conflict arose among them, resulting in harm to all junior creation. Using this tradition, Tolkien gives his account of creation in the first part of *The Silmarillion*, "The Music of the Ainur."

The idea of music as the instrument of creation is not a primitive idea but a Platonic one, from *Timaeus* again; compare the singing in Job quoted above. As Dryden put it, "From harmony, from heavenly harmony / This universal frame began" ("Song for Saint Cecilia's Day, 1687"). Tolkien makes clear that creation is the work of the One, Ilúvatar; but the Ainur, each from a different part of His infinite mind, add their proper qualities to the music which He then brings into being as our universe.

It is hard to imagine how an angel in the intimacy of the Creator could throw itself out of the divine order, but evidently that order has been warped. Tolkien's account of the origin of evil says: "it came into the heart of Melkor to interweave matters of his own imagining that were not in accord with the theme of Ilúvatar; for he sought therein to increase the power and glory of the part assigned to himself" (*S*, 16). In other words, the first sin was pride, the idolatry of one's own beauty rather than the humility of seeing it within God's order.

The Creator's method of bringing good out of intended evil is shown in His conversation with Ulmo, Lord of Waters:

"Seest thou not how . . . Melkor hath made war upon thy province? He hath bethought him of bitter cold immoderate, and yet hath not destroyed the beauty of thy fountains, nor of thy clear pools. Behold the snow, and the cunning work of frost! Melkor hath devised heats and fire without restraint, and hath not dried up thy desire nor utterly quelled the music of the sea. Behold rather the height and glory of the clouds, and the everchanging mists; and listen to the fall of rain upon the Earth! . . ."
Then Ulmo answered: "Truly, Water is become now fairer than my heart imagined." (*S*, 19)

And so, Tolkien says, all evil ultimately will be turned to greater beauty.

The second section of the book tells of the archangelic powers, Valar, who chose to dwell in this world when the Creator gave it being. Readers can have endless fun connecting them with the panthea of polytheistic religions. Eight are chief among them: Manwë, Lord of the Air; Varda (Elbereth), Lady of the Stars, his consort; Ulmo, Lord of Waters; Yavanna, Lady of Plants; Aulë, Lord of Earth, her consort; Mandos, Lord of the Halls of the Dead; Nienna, Lady of Sorrow, his sister; and Oromë, Lord of the Hunt. Melkor, the enemy, also came to the new world. With both him and the Valar were Maiar, subordinate beings, "angels" to their "archangels." The wisest Maia was Olorin, whom readers of Tolkien's previously published works know as Gandalf (II, 353). Some of Melkor's Maiar were Balrogs, which finally explains why one was a match for Gandalf in *The Fellowship of the Ring*.

The middle and longest section of the book turns on the history of the Silmarils. The history of Middle-earth can be traced by that of light. While the world was a disk on the encircling sea, the Valar made two lamps to illuminate it all and dwelt in the middle where the lights blended. Melkor burrowed underground and overthrew the lamps, causing the first cataclysm and marring the earth's symmetry. The Valar moved west out of Middle-earth, across the Great Sea. There in Valinor, Yavanna sang the Two Trees to life, whose flowers shed silver and gold light. Days began to be counted by their blossoms' opening and closing: "days" which to us would be epochs. Some of the light was mounted by Fëanor, greatest of elven craftsmen, in the three jewels, the Silmarilli. Their beauty drew his inordinate love and also the envy of Melkor. He, with Ungoliant (spider in form, by nature probably maia, S, 73), killed the Trees, and of their light was made "a Darkness that seemed not lack but a thing with being of its own: for it was indeed made by malice out of Light, and it had power to pierce the eye, and . . . strangle the very will" (S, 76).

As scientists say darkness is not a thing in itself but only the absence of light, so theologians say evil has no being of its own, but is only the privation of good. But to our perceptions in everyday life, darkness and evil appear to have being. Tolkien is saying that the apparent being of evil—in the story, of darkness—comes from the personal energy of its agent plus the existence of the substance on which the agent acts; which personal energy and existence can only derive from the Creator, however the creature misuses them. It has been said that the problem of evil is the only real question in theology; in this passage Tolkien treats the question more theoretically than usual. In his more leisurely narratives, evil is just found as part of life in this world, and the question is how one deals with it.

Melkor escaped with the three Silmarilli and was dubbed Morgoth, the Black Enemy. Now Valinor, like Middle-earth, was lit only by stars. But in the Trees' last throes, they bore a flower and a fruit which the Valar set two Maiar to sailing round the world as the Sun and Moon. Their light checked Morgoth for a while.[19]

While the Trees lit Valinor and the stars Middle-earth, the Elves awoke: the first of two races whom the Ainur had foreseen and called the "children of Ilúvatar," because they were younger (created later) and weaker than the Ainur. The second such race was Mankind. Varda made new stars for the Elves, who loved them and her ever after (cf. chapter 4, note 13).

Melkor captured some Elves near the time of their beginning, and they "were put . . . in prison, and by slow arts of cruelty were corrupted and enslaved; and thus did Melkor breed the hideous race of the Orcs. . . . [N]aught that had life . . . could ever Melkor make. . . . [D]eep in their dark hearts the Orcs loathed the Master whom they served in fear, the maker only of their misery. This it may be was the vilest deed of Melkor" (S, 50). So the Orcs are explained: a race which has been adversely remarked on because of its total depravity. Melkor was responsible for everything but their being. For the Elves' sake, the Valar attacked and bound Melkor and invited the Elves to the West. Then arose the division of light and dark elves already mentioned, because some did not go to the light of the Trees; Melkor had sown mistrust of the Valar.

Foreseeing the children of Ilúvatar and impatient for the beautiful world to be inhabited, Aulë the Smith had tried to make a sentient race: a deed potentially Melkor-like. But Aulë realized that his power would only extend to making a race of automata, not persons; and recognizing his foolishness, he submitted the things to Ilúvatar and offered to break them. The Creator, seeing his humility, granted them free will instead and a place in His plan. This was the origin of the Dwarves; it looks like Tolkien's response to the suggestion of misbirth in the word "Nephilim/Nibelung."

Tolkien does not deal in any detail with the beginnings of the human race, presumably because Genesis has. Mankind has "strange gifts," mysterious even to the Ainur. The creator "willed that the hearts of Men should seek beyond the world and should find no rest therein;[20] but they should have a virtue to shape their life . . . beyond the Music of the Ainur, which is as fate to all things else. . . . The children of Men dwell only a short space in the world alive, and are not bound to it, and depart soon whither the Elves know not. . . . Death is their fate, the gift of Ilúvatar. . . . But Melkor has cast his shadow upon it" (S, 41–42). The odd brevity of the human life span on this planet has been noted in other mythologies; one wonders whether it might be connected with Jesus's enigmatic remark about "days shortened for the sake of God's chosen" (Matthew 24:22). Tolkien keeps repeating, to himself as well as to us, that death for human beings is a gift of their loving Creator; sadly though he feels the "shadow" of fear and loneliness with which people tend to regard it.[21]

Shortly after the rising of the Sun the human race began. Some made friends with the Dark Elves still in Middle-earth, and some moved westward into Beleriand—the part of Middle-earth closest to Valinor—while Morgoth, with the stolen Silmarils, fortified a hold in the North.

He was pursued back to Middle-earth against the counsel of the Valar by an army of Elves (Noldor) under Fëanor, who bound himself with a vow of vengeance, such as has propelled much of the world's tragic literature. Galadriel was among the host. On the shore of Middle-earth they routed Morgoth's forces; but Fëanor was killed, leaving the rash vow on his seven sons.

Thereafter the history becomes more and more involved, as the returned Noldor meet various groups of Moriquendi, Men, and Dwarves. War, battle, treachery, and suspicion wash over

Beleriand from the Falas to the Ered Luin, from Hithlum to the
Isle of Balar, in accordance with the prophecy of Mandos to
the departing Noldor: "Tears unnumbered shall ye shed. . . . On
the House of Fëanor the wrath of the Valar lieth . . . and upon all
that will follow them. . . . Their Oath shall drive them, and yet
betray them, and ever snatch away the very treasures that they
have sworn to pursue. To evil shall all things turn that they begin
well; and by treason of kin unto kin, and the fear of treason,
shall this come to pass" (S, 88). This utterance is called the Curse
of Mandos, but the unfolding of the story shows that it is not a
punishment: it is simply a statement of the consequences—dire—
which the elven-host's rash action will draw after it.

Tolkien's narration in *The Silmarillion* is very condensed, by
contrast with his thoroughness in *The Lord of the Rings*. He
gives biblically brief accounts of stories which would fill a whole
modern novel, such as the love of Elwë the Elf and Melian the
Maia, the ill-starred marriage of Eol and Aredhel, or the friendship of Fingon and Maedhros. Such is Tolkien's authority that
one has the impression of seeing in the smith Eol the *source* for
Vulcan, Wayland, or Ilmarinen; or in Maedhros on the rock that
of Prometheus or Loki's punishment, not to mention Blondel
finding Richard Lionheart. There are several theses-worth of
mythic motifs in *The Silmarillion*. On two stories Tolkien spreads
himself more than the rest: those of Turin and Beren.

Turin is the dragon slayer and the man caught in unwitting
incest; his family was cursed by Morgoth, like other fabled lines.
Fostered by Elves, Turin flees to live with outlawed men and
the dwarf Mîm (Norse name). Betrayed to Orcs, he is rescued
by his faithful friend—whom Turin in confusion at once kills.
The curse works. Turin joins Finrod's Elves until they are attacked by Morgoth's first fire-drake, Glaurung, the worst of
Tolkien's dragons. Turin looks into his eyes and listens to his
words, "and he saw himself as in a mirror misshapen by malice,
and loathed that which he saw" (S, 214). In Turin's life he has
done some unquestionable ill, and also considerable good. The
fiendish perception which Glaurung conveys to his mind stains
all the good with doubt and disgust.[22]

Glaurung holds Turin until the Elf-maid who loves him has
been led away, then sends him on a wild-goose chase after his

mother and sister, while the dragon settles down on the Elves' treasure. When Turin's mother and sister try to find him, Glaurung strikes Nienor, the sister, with amnesia. She is found without faculties by Turin, who eventually marries her, and she conceives a child.

Glaurung threatens their land and Turin stabs him underneath with his sword of meteorite-iron. The dragon has only sufficient breath to tell Nienor who her husband is, whereupon she leaps to her and the baby's death in the ravine. Once the story is clear to Turin, he throws himself on the sword. In this tale, Tolkien condenses all the near-despair of pre-Christian tragedy from every mythology he knew.[23] "As flies to wanton boys are we to the gods; They kill us for their sport."

Beren and Luthien's story, however, is of triumph beyond hope. He was the first human being to set foot in Doriath, the wood ruled by Luthien's father Elwë Thingol and guarded by the enchantment of her mother Melian the Maia. Beren saw and loved Luthien, as told in the poem quoted in chapter 1. Thingol, loath to give his daughter to a mortal man, set as her bride-price a Silmaril; the three jewels were then in Morgoth's crown on his head in the fortress of Angband. Tolkien in his own life was familiar with the stern deferment of a marriage; not only he and Edith, but his own parents, had had to defer their wedding by the order of a father (figure) until the younger partner was twenty-one. Thingol thus involved his inviolate realm in the hostilities of Middle-earth. Beren was captured by Morgoth's lieutenant Sauron (a Maia) and put into a pit where a werewolf ate his companions one by one.[24]

Luthien, resolved to rescue him, escaped her father's imprisonment by climbing down a rope of her hair; but she was captured by Celegorm and Curufin, sons of Fëanor still bound by his vow that *no one* should have a Silmaril but themselves. Celegorm's hound, a gift from Oromë, rescued Luthien. To reach Beren, he fought the shape-shifting Sauron, who finally surrendered rather than be sent naked, bodiless, back to Morgoth.

Forestalling Celegorm and Curufin's attempt to kidnap Luthien, Beren leaves her safe at home and sets out again for Angband. But Luthien and the hound, disguised as bat and wolf, persist in accompanying him. Here is one of Tolkien's female characters who will not settle down to be protected (see chapter 6). Their fate, says the dog, is "hopeless, yet not certain" (S, 179). The theme of continuing with no feeling of hope recurs in Tolkien's stories.[25]

At the gate of Angband lies Carcharoth, a wolf to rank with Fenris, Cerberus, or the Eskimo hell-dog. Luthien's word casts him into sleep. She sings before Morgoth, an active Euridice,[26] and even the Dark Enemy falls to her song. Beren slices a jewel from his crown. Alas, as they flee, Carcharoth snaps off Beren's hand, Silmaril and all. The holy jewel scorches his insides, maddening him. Eagles—rescuers in early as in late ages—carry the lovers back to Doriath as the wrath of Angband erupts. At last Thingol betrothes them. One wonders whether, in Tolkien's mind, the modern custom of giving one's fiancée a diamond—most sparkling of this world's gems—goes back to a faded memory of Beren and Luthien's silmaril.

The wolf approaches Thingol's borders; in the ensuing hunt Carcharoth, the hound, and Beren are all killed. Luthien dies of grief, as Elves can. But, says Tolkien, the Lay of Release from Bondage does not end.

Beren's human spirit does not leave the world, but waits in the Halls of Mandos; and the Lord of the Dead, too, is moved by Luthien's song. She is granted either to dwell with the Valar or to live a mortal life in Middle-earth. She chooses the latter, and Beren and Luthien have a second private life in Middle-earth. Their son is Dior and his daughter Elwing, who gave the Silmaril to her husband Earendil the mariner, now the Morning Star.

Beren and Luthien's marriage was the first of Tolkien's three elf-human matches, the others being the marriages of Tuor and Idril, Aragorn and Arwen. Tolkien has two races called "children of God" which can marry; and unlike Genesis, he has the human partner be the male. Maiar can marry elves, as shown by the single case of Melian and Thingol, and therefore could presumably intermarry with human beings too. Orcs, being ruined elves, would breed the same way, and indeed Saruman during the War of the Ring appears to have developed an orc-human half-breed (I, 244; II, 96, 180, 218); Tolkien mercifully never makes his method clear.[27]

Hobbits would also be cross-fertile with these other beings. It has been speculated that hobbits and human beings started intermarrying at Bree, and that both are our ancestors.[28] The rumor of a hobbit-"fairy" match (see chapter 4, p. 67) remains puzzling. Tolkien disliked the modern trivial use of "fairy," and generally avoided the word (cf. "On Fairy Stories"). Possibly "fairy" was used for "elf" by provincial hobbits who did not believe in elves; or possibly some kind of nymph was envisaged. Anyway, Tolkien himself brands the rumor "absurd" (*H*, 16, rev. ed.).

Tolkien never uses the word nymph; but Goldberry is the daughter of the river-woman of the Withywindle, which must make them nymphs (females) of either *genii loci* (place-spirits) or elementals.[29] Conceivably the river-woman might have been a maia of Ulmo's. Goldberry—her name comes from the romance of Havelok the Dane—is married to Tom Bombadil, who is a—————?: Tom's nature is perplexing. His wearing boots proves him no hobbit; Tolkien maddeningly describes him as "a man, or so it seemed. At any rate he was too large and heavy for a hobbit, if not quite tall enough for one of the Big People [human beings]" (I, 168). Knowing that Tom was originally Michael Tolkien's Dutch doll does us singularly little good within the story. He is most like a combination of Pan and the unfallen Adam, and will be further discussed in chapter 6. Tolkien's mythic history shows how biblical and other mythologies might have been grounded.

Earendil alone of human beings reaches Valinor, to beg the Valar's forgiveness for the tragedy-meshed children of Ilúvatar. They send him and the Silmaril voyaging as a star of hope. So in *The Silmarillion* we have the full prose story of the "flammifer of Westernesse" whom Bilbo had the nerve to sing of among his son Elrond's elves (I, 308ff.).

Having heard Earendil's story, the Valar (with the Elves of Valinor) go and overthrow Morgoth, breaking up the whole North, which to this day is a frozen waste—though now, in our Christian era, said to be inhabited by Father Christmas. So again does evil give place to merriment.

The Enemy is thrust out of the universe of time. The remaining two Silmarils are stolen by Fëanor's last two sons; but burned by the jewels, the Elves cast them into the depths of the earth and the sea. Thus earth, water, and air, each element but fire, has its jewel.

Human beings fought on both sides of this War of Wrath; Tolkien continues their history in "Akallabêth," the next section of the book. Those who helped the Valar were granted an island, Numenor, between Middle-earth and the Undying Lands. Its people lived long and learned much; their only check was a ban on sailing west out of sight of Numenor. Sailing east, they helped the benighted human beings of Middle-earth, who took them for gods; but later the Numenorians seized dominion and exacted tribute; here Tolkien hooks onto Plato's *Timaeus*.

Their degeneration stemmed from fear of death and consequent jealousy of immortals. Tolkien, once told that his books were "about" power, said oh, he thought they were about Death and the desire for deathlessness.[30] Having been left behind alive in Middle-earth so much himself, he would naturally regard death with interest, and with longing and resentment, as well as human nervousness of the unfamiliar. In "On Fairy Stories" he remarks that while our tales often recount the Escape from Death, "The Human-stories of the elves are doubtless full of the Escape from Deathlessness" (*TR*, 67). Elves are supernatural, says Tolkien, only if super is taken as an intensive: their nature and their entire destiny—by contrast to humans'—are bound up with the planet they inhabit.

The Numenorians could not have imagined deathlessness as a fate to be escaped. Their fear of death and envy of the immortals were fomented by Sauron, brought back to Numenor a supposed captive to make Middle-earth safe. Speaking in the King's ear, Sauron undermined all the godly practices of the island. At last King Ar-Pharazôn set sail for the Undying Lands, breaking the ban. When he stepped on the shore, "the Valar laid down their Guardianship and called upon the One" (III, 392).

He responded by rolling the world into a sphere, with the Undying Lands removed from its surface. To reach them, one would have to sail off on a tangent. Tolkien imagined that certain people had found such a "straight road" from accounts like the voyage of Saint Brendan, which he adapted in his poem "Imram" (Gaelic, "voyage").[31] As the seas are bent, landmasses rip apart and waves overwhelm Numenor. A few of its people faithful to the Valar had embarked and were blown to Middle-earth, bringing seven seeing-stones (palantiri) and a sapling of the desecrated White Tree.

The fifth section of *The Silmarillion* recapitulates the history of the Rings of Power, already mostly known to readers of *The Lord of the Rings.*

Set as it is before Christ or even Abraham, *The Silmarillion* is a book about things getting worse and worse. "If it has passed from the high and beautiful to darkness and ruin, that was of old the fate of [the World] Marred" (S, 255).

C. S. Lewis in *That Hideous Strength* says, "Good is always getting better and bad is always getting worse: the possibilities of even apparent neutrality are always diminishing. The whole thing is sorting itself out all the time, coming to a point, getting sharper and harder."[32] Tolkien's account of the world shows the opposite process: as time passes, the "best" deeds get more and more admixture of ill and tragedy. People land themselves in predicaments they never should have caused, then display all sorts of excellence in enduring the consequences. Hatred and love both bring doom.

The Silmarillion contains little of Tolkien's poetry, by contrast to *The Hobbit* and *The Lord of the Rings.* Some of the stories exist in verse, and we can hope that Christopher will publish them eventually. Then future scholars can ponder the *Poetic* and *Prose Silmarillion* as we do the *Poetic* and *Prose Edda.*

Last published of his major works, *The Silmarillion* does what Tolkien later mocked himself for undertaking: it is "a body of more or less connected legend, ranging from the large and cosmogonic to the level of romantic fairy-story.... The cycles should be linked to a majestic whole, and yet leave scope for other minds and hands, wielding paint and music and drama."[33] He shows the "sources" for motifs from Ceres and Sigurd to Rapunzel and Mother Carey; but instead of a mere catalog, the book is an edifice, giving coherence to scattered, ambiguous bits of lore and fact. It is Tolkien's book about the world.

CHAPTER 6

The Dawn of the Age of Man

TOLKIEN wanted his mythic history published. Allen and Unwin were pressing him for more hobbit stories. Many juvenile authors wrote series.[1] Even with only *The Hobbit* published, it was evident that Tolkien had enough of a world to put out a book for the Christmas trade annually for a decade or so (as Lewis was to do with the seven Narnia books). Plots and additional characters could be mined from folklore and old literature as needed, since the author obviously enjoyed such mining. Let the professor crank out the manuscripts.

Not J. R. R. Tolkien. Writing was not his daily-bread activity: that was lecturing, tutorials, and marking tests, as well as departmental administrative work. Writing was for himself, his family, or his friends. Yet he did know and love hobbits and their setting, and of course was pleased that his juvenile was a success. So he agreed to keep on, but wrote to Stanley Unwin, "what more can hobbits do? They can be comic, but their comedy is suburban unless it is set against things more elemental."[2]

He fiddled round for weeks, then months, with birthday parties, quests for more gold, Bilbo's son Bingo, and a "queer-looking brown-faced hobbit" named Trotter.[3] But he did realize that his juvenile had "got drawn into the edge" of his *Silmarillion* mythology. He knew, though the reader could not, that "the Necromancer," who Gandalf said was too much for the dwarves (*H*, 37), was Sauron: Morgoth's lieutenant, Beren's tormentor, Numenor's underminer. His presence in Middle-earth would indeed give Gandalf greater concerns than Thorin and Company. It also dawned on Tolkien that more could be done with the the ring of invisibility. Why was it under a mountain? Perhaps it came from the Necromancer? Did it do anything besides make one invisible? While one was invisible in this world, where did

94

one show? The ring was not safe, Tolkien realized: "You must either lose it, or *yourself*."[4]

Now he had a story like *The Hobbit* but different: provincial hobbits leave home on an errand which began as someone else's story: but this quest is not to gain a treasure, but to lose one. Something *is* to be done about the Necromancer, as Thorin overweeningly suggested. Finally it occurred to Tolkien that the ring was the Ring, vehicle of much of Sauron's power; if he regained it, he could rule all rings and the world.[5] As Carpenter observes, now Tolkien had his story, but it was not a juvenile. It was a part he had not planned of his mythic history, between the fall of Numenor and the history we know, that of the age of man. He could have announuced his subject-matter like the author of the *Nibelungenlied*: "Of joys and celebrations, of weeping and of mourning, / Of valiant heroes' battles now hear the wondrous story."

Like Thomas Aquinas and the Bible, we can read Tolkien's stories on a historical level, but also in other ways, including applying the tales to the individual personality. The personal application of the Quest has already been indicated: it is considered the story of the hero's initiation into maturity.[6] A quest is to gain and then share something, and every human being must achieve and share adulthood.

In *The Lord of the Rings* much maturing is done by various characters; but the quest Tolkien gives us is to *lose* something. If one will read myths as personal documents, is there something which every human being must lose? Yes; bitterly though he hates to part with it, he cannot thrive by clinging to it: his life in Middle-earth. In Tolkien's belief, what we call the end of life is an even greater initiation than reaching maturity.

One hears of people who stand foursquare; Tolkien's work stands three-triangular. *The Hobbit* and *The Silmarillion* can be pictured as equal but far-apart base angles, *The Lord of the Rings* as the apex where a line from each intersects the other.

Allen and Unwin, hoping for a hobbit series, were left standing, and the seventeen-year gap occurred in Tolkien's fiction, not filled to speak of by the publication of *Farmer Giles of Ham* in 1949. Tolkien kept foreseeing the end of his story, and more events kept piling in before it. His mind became distressed and cured itself with "Leaf by Niggle" (see chapter 3 above).

On a framework like *The Hobbit*'s in a world descended from that of *The Silmarillion*, Tolkien worked out line by line a story like both and neither. While *The Hobbit* shows the avenging of a private wrong and the maturing of one hobbit, *The Lord of the Rings* shows the prevention of a global wrong and the maturing of persons of several races; one race, the human, is now prepared to take over the governance of Middle-earth. While the *Silmarillion* as we have it chronicles more than two ages in one moderate-sized volume, *The Lord of the Rings* details a year's journey in more than twice the space.

The work is divided into six books of about ten chapters each: (1) The First Journey; (2) The Journey of the Nine Companions; (3) The Treason of Isengard; (4) The Journey of the Ring-bearers; (5) The War of the Ring; (6) The End of the Third Age. Tolkien wrote to a student, "Of course, the present division into Volumes, mere practical necessity of publication, is a falsification. As is shown by the unsatisfactory titles of the last two volumes. The work is in no legitimate literary sense a 'trilogy.' . . . The only units of any structural significance are the 'books.' "[7] Allen and Unwin first divided the work into three volumes so they could print fewer of each successive one, forsooth. Of their titles, *The Fellowship of the Ring* is all right; *The Two Towers* is unclear (though it sounds fine—there are five towers in the story); and *The Return of the King* gives away too much. Because of the three volumes, the story is often considered a trilogy. In fact, ever since Tolkien did not write a trilogy, the fantasy trilogy has been a form well recognized by readers and publishers.[8]

"The First Journey" takes the Ring and Frodo Baggins (Bilbo's nephew) to Rivendell, with more detail and danger than Bilbo and the dwarves had. Bilbo vanishes from the Shire by means of the Ring, which Gandalf reminds him to leave for his heir. Of course, says Bilbo, heading out the door with it. Without his awareness, the Ring has grown an adhesive grip on his spirit: only under threat can he wrench away from it. Yet he is partly relieved not to have it. His hate-attachment to the Ring foreshadows its effects later in the story. Tolkien is setting himself a situation in which greed brings even more danger than does ordinary gold-lust in his other works.

Some twenty years later, when Frodo is about fifty (Bilbo's age in *The Hobbit*), Gandalf returns from researches on rings. A mortal who keeps a Great Ring "does not die, but he does not grow or obtain more life, he merely continues. . . . And if he often uses the Ring to make himself invisible, he *fades* . . . and walks in the twilight under the eye of the dark power that rules the Rings" (I, 76). That the Baggins ring is the ruling Ring is confirmed by its inscription: "One Ring to rule them all, One Ring to find them, / One Ring to bring them all and in the darkness bind them" (I, 81). This, rule without consent, is the desire of Sauron, who now seeks his Ring from his dark tower in Mordor, some thousand miles southeast from Hobbiton.

Gandalf has found out the history of Gollum, formerly Sméagol (Old English, "worming in," same root as Smaug and smial): he murdered for the Ring, "because the gold looked so bright and beautiful" (I, 85). That he hungered for beauty and not for power, and also the modesty of his use of the Ring— first for eavesdropping, later for catching food—explains why Gollum survived his long tenure as well as he did: "tougher than even one of the Wise would have guessed. . . . Certainly he had never 'faded.' He is thin and tough still" (I, 86–87).

Part of Tolkien's characterization of Gollum leads one to suspect his artist-self of taking a slap at his scholar-self: "interested in roots and beginnings," burrowing under trees instead of looking up at their leaves (I, 84). For Tolkien's fiction, though, his knowledge of every cell from roottip to leaftip is part of his sequoial merit.

The Precious lost, Gollum crept out in search of Baggins, since Bilbo had told his name. Gollum became the origin of vampire legends in Mirkwood (I, 91) and was taken and tortured in Mordor. Now Sauron knows the name Baggins. Frodo cries, "What a pity Bilbo did not stab the vile creature, when he had a chance!" (I, 92).

The reader is not allowed to agree. "Pity? It was Pity that stayed his hand. Pity, and mercy: not to strike without need. . . . Deserves [death]! I daresay [Gollum] does. Many that live deserve death. And some that die deserve life. Can you give it to them?" (I, 92–93). Like Chaucer, Tolkien values the virtue of pity more highly than is the fashion of our time.[9] Tolkien has been called a warmonger, but a reading of his whole work

shows pity and mercy turning out far more important than
military derring-do, though circumstances may demand the
latter too.[10]

Gandalf tells Frodo that Sauron is summoning the Ring, and
it too is an agent: "A Ring of Power looks after itself" (I, 87).
Opponents too great for a hobbit; but Gandalf hints at a third
agency. "I can put it no plainer than by saying that Bilbo was
meant to find the Ring, and *not* by its maker . . . an encouraging
thought" (I, 88). What Gandalf knows but Tolkien never
states is the care of Providence for the world. In the Third Age,
creatures younger than the Valar and Maiar had had no direct
dealings with the Creator, and Tolkien scrupulously sticks to
a mind-set possible before Abraham, even if hobbits do have
teakettles and tobacco.

Having learned all this, Frodo offers the Ring to Gandalf.
"No!" cries the wizard. "Do not tempt me! For I do not wish to
become like the Dark Lord himself" (I, 95). Gandalf, a maia,
would have the power to wield the Ring; in fact he already bears
one of the three elf-rings. But he sees and steadfastly fears the
consequences of taking the One, however good the wielder's
original motive. Others are put through the same temptation as
the story goes on; Aragorn, Galadriel, and Faramir are three
more who resist.

Winding up his long exposition, Gandalf warns Frodo, "be
careful of what you say, even to your best friend! The enemy
has many spies" (I, 97). Suddenly he plucks up Sam Gamgee,
Frodo's gardener's boy, who appears a quintessential dumb
rustic: "Mr. Frodo, sir! . . . Don't let him turn me into anything
unnatural!" (I, 97).

This scene has several layers, in a way characteristic of Tolkien.
The reader's nerves, like Frodo's, are strung up by hearing about
the menace of Sauron; warned of spies, we find an eavesdropper—
it gives us a nasty qualm. Similar qualms occur on meeting the
cross Farmer Maggot, seeing birds overhead, and entering Fangorn Wood; and when the silent cloaked man in the inn eyes
Frodo becoming overjolly.[11] Tolkien has been both praised and
damned for making his good and bad characters too clear; but
for suspense he makes great use of readers' and characters' uncertainty, batting them between the sinister and the homely.

We are alarmed at Sam's advent, then relieved when Gandalf looks him over and says he shall go with Frodo. Frodo tells Sam, "if you really care about me, you will keep this dead secret. See?" (I, 98). This order overlies another layer of Tolkien's plot, revealed in chapter 5, "A Conspiracy Unmasked" (qualm). Sam does care for Frodo: very much indeed; and for that very reason he does reveal his master's secret to three of Frodo's cousins. The overdone hayseed was a mask for a most capable companion.

Frodo's heroism throughout the story impresses characters and readers alike; but he could not and by mercy need not act alone. The other hobbits have even less clue than he of their danger, but because they are his friends—friendship matters to Tolkien—they stick with him.

Sam reaches such stature that some have agitated for his being the real hero.[12] Tolkien said, "My 'Sam Gamgee' is indeed a reflexion of the English soldier, of the privates and batmen I knew in the 1914 war, and recognized as so far superior to myself."[13] Yet a visitor to Tolkien found the author sounding hostile: "Tolkien spoke to me about Sam as 'vulgar' and 'despicable,' and . . . sententious and cocksure. 'He was the youngest son of a stupid and conceited old peasant. Together with his loyal master-servant attitude, and his personal love for Frodo, he retains a touch of the contempt of his kind (moderated to tolerant pity) for motives above their reach.' "[14] Kilby sets this hostility next to Tolkien's expressed disgust with George Macdonald, to whom Tolkien's fiction actually owes a considerable debt. Lewis mentions Macdonald's quality of "good death."[15] It seems that Tolkien was crotchety at seventy-four and quite likely resenting dependence on any person or kind of person.[16]

The Ring will be sent to the only place where it can be destroyed: the Cracks of Doom (Tolkien is punning again). Frodo, Sam, and Pippin set out without Gandalf's promised escort. A sinister big person in black is inquiring for Baggins as they leave, and on the journey similar Black Riders overtake them; Tolkien had not planned these characters.[17] They turn out to be the wraiths of men who bore the nine rings for humankind.

A party of elves treats the hobbits to a small edition of

the feasts in Mirkwood in *The Hobbit*. Sam, who has been longing to meet elves, finds them "quite different from what I expected—so old and young, so gay and sad, as it were" (I, 126–27). His sensitivity increases Frodo's respect.

Frodo pretends to move to the hobbits' eastern border, but really leaves the Shire the next morning, with "conspirators" Sam, Pippin, and Merry. Black Riders watching the road, the hobbits start through the Old Forest. Dearly though Tolkien loves trees, it is a menacing place, breathing of Arthur Rackham and the Ash in Macdonald's *Phantastes*. Old Man Willow nearly traps the hobbits. Michael Tolkien used to hide in the crack of an old willow near Oxford, which doubtless gave his father the idea.[18] Frodo aimlessly but providentially cries "Help!"

Singing and dancing along comes that doll turned mystery, Tom Bombadil, and commands the willow to let its victims loose. The poem "The Adventures of Tom Bombadil" shows more of his apparently careless power: terrors turn nearly into comedies in his sight, including the Ring. Tom and Goldberry's house had the antidote for all the travelers' nightmare fears. The hobbits' dreams show both ordinary sleeping mental processes and special visions; Tolkien knows both.

He writes little about marriage, sometimes about marriage marred (ents and entwives, Turin and Nienor, Aotrou and Itroun); but in Tom and Goldberry he sketches an ideal match. The "hobbits sat half in wonder and half in laughter; so fair was the grace of Goldberry and so merry and odd the caperings of Tom. Yet in some fashion they seemed to weave a single dance, neither hindering the other . . . and with great speed food and vessels and lights were set in order" (I, 183). A dance is a leading old symbol for cosmic harmony.

Frodo tries twice, as the reader would like to, to ask who Tom is. Goldberry says, "Master of wood, water and hill," but not their owner: "all things growing or living in the land belong each to themselves" (I, 174). This makes Tom another steward, like Denethor and Gandalf (cf. III, 33f.). [19] All Tom will say about himself is, "Eldest. . . . Tom was here already, before the seas were bent. He knew the dark under the stars when it was fearless—before the Dark Lord [Morgoth, not Sauron] came from Outside" (I, 182).

Tom appears to be Tolkien's gloss on the description of primordial Wisdom: "The Lord created me in the beginning of His ways. . . . I was playing before Him at all times, playing in the World."[20] This biblical connection puts Tom's unparalleled levity in a new light. In having him the consort of the nymph Goldberry, singer of the rain, Tolkien shows his ideal as a union of consciousness with nature; hence the shining forth of cosmic harmony in their household.

The hobbits, after leaving Tom's, are caught in a barrow. These burial mounds had been raised for descendants of Numenorians; in his trance, Merry "becomes" such a defeated warrior. The graves became haunted by the ghosts of their opponents, followers of the Witch-king of Angmar, who is now the chief ring-wraith. The barrow-wight does not seem to be after the Ring, but only to crave death and cold for all. Still, if he caught Frodo, no doubt Angmar would get the Ring and then Sauron would.

But "a seed of courage" sprouts in Frodo, as it can in any hobbit (I, 194); and his will stiffens when his might is least: Maldon syndrome. He defends his friends and summons Tom. Bombadil, because "His songs are stronger" (I, 196), exorcises the wight, and exposes the treasure to fresh air and sharing, breaking its spell. The hobbits are given daggers; Merry's will have its revenge on Angmar (III, 143, 146). Tom will not pass his own borders: good powerful people are not empire builders.

The travelers reach Bree, a unique village of men and hobbits both.[21] A dark figure climbs in over the gate after them (qualm). At the inn Frodo puts on the Ring: a cause for rumor. The hobbits are joined, whether they will or no, by the grim-looking ranger Strider; he requests that they take him as guide to Rivendell.

Sam does not trust him, foreshadowing Sam's later feelings toward Gollum. Gollum really is untrustworthy; but Sam, as Frodo's most devoted henchman, can hardly bear any other guide, however needed. Two traits about Strider seem reassuring: his humor about his own looks and his refusal to foment suspicion against the innkeeper: "No, I don't think any harm of old Butterbur. Only he does not altogether like mysterious vagabonds of my sort" (I, 224). Veritable bad guys do foment suspicion.

The landlord, however good his intentions, has failed to forward a note to Frodo from Gandalf, advising his departure before the Black Riders had come. The note says Strider is Aragorn, whom Gandalf had mentioned as "the greatest traveller and huntsman of this age of the world" (I, 91). "All that is gold does not glitter," writes Tolkien, playing with proverbs again (I, 231).

Hobbits and Ranger journey, camp, and are refreshed with old tales including a song of Beren and Luthien, whose story has special significance for Aragorn as well as Tolkien. Black Riders attack, and the urge to put on the Ring overcomes Frodo; as he becomes invisible in the ordinary world, he and the wraiths can see each other clearly. One knifes him. Frodo invokes Elbereth. His wound chills him almost fatally, though Aragorn helps all he can with leaves of athelas. Later we learn that the herb is "Life to the dying, / in the king's hand lying" (III, 172). The weatherbeaten ranger is in fact the King, as dawns on a reader with gradual surprise.

Passing Bilbo's trolls, Sam sings "The Stone Troll," which he made up. Frodo says, " 'I am learning a lot about Sam Gamgee. . . . First he was a conspirator, now he's a jester. He'll end up by becoming a wizard—or a warrior!' 'I hope not,' said Sam" (I, 278). He does: a warrior in the orc-tower of Cirith Ungol, a wizard in restoring fertility to the Shire. After Tolkien had written the story, he rewrote it backward, weaving in rich use of foreshadowing.

An elf appears and aids their dash through the ford to Rivendell under the noses of the Nine. Frodo, nearly faded by his wound, resists with surprising courage. So ends "The First Journey."

Gandalf and Bilbo are both found at the Last Homely House, where a great council provides more exposition. Gandalf has been held prisoner by the chief wizard Saruman (Old English, "crafty man"), who now craves the Ring and marshals beautiful arguments against Gandalf's.[22]

Elrond's daughter Arwen is at Rivendell. A first-time reader is unlikely to pick up the love between her and Aragorn, though Strider has told Frodo that his heart is at Rivendell (I, 270), and Bilbo expects them to be together: "Why weren't you at the feast? The Lady Arwen was there" (I, 307).[23] Only later do we find out about their devotion.

Elrond, like Elwë before him, did not want his daughter marrying a mortal; if she did, it should be none less than the King of the North and South Kingdoms. This fairy-tale forbidding father jars a little in Tolkien's story—until one learns of Father Morgan's thwarting Tolkien's relationship with Edith. Throughout the story, Aragorn's relation to Arwen is one kind of courtly love: not the pining, fainting kind, but that in which the thought of his *haulte amie* ("lofty beloved") upholds the lover through dangers and discouragements. Arwen is scarcely characterized, but her presence as a figure gives a resonance to the whole story: puts a further motive behind Aragorn's perseverance and rounds out the restoring of the kingdom. War is but a phase; marriage is part of the necessary achievement.[24]

The upshot of the council is the title of the second book, "The Journey of the Nine Companions." Frodo volunteers to carry the Ring on, in the wan hope of destroying it. Tolkien says, "such is oft the course of deeds that move the wheels of the world: small hands do them because they must, while the eyes of the great are elsewhere" (I, 353).

Sam will go with him, Merry and Pippin, Strider and Gandalf. Since Gandalf is a maia, his companions are in the position of Tobias led by Raphael. A second human being in the company is Boromir, son of the ruling Steward of Gondor, come to Rivendell in answer to a dream which the reader knows points to Aragorn and Frodo. Boromir's concern is that his city, Minas Tirith, shall have sufficient military might to continue resisting Sauron; so far, he says, they are the sole and unthanked defenders. Eighth of the Nine Walkers is the dwarf Gimli, son of Gloin (from *The Hobbit*), come for counsel because Black Riders had been asking round Erebor for Baggins and a trifling ring. Ninth is the elf Legolas, son of Thranduil, come with the news that Gollum has escaped their guard. Gloin still smarts at the memory of his imprisonment by Thranduil (I, 355), and the relations of their sons are chilly.

The company, representing nearly all free races, sets out on December 25, from which a Christian reader can take more hope than the characters feel. Elrond counsels them, "You will meet

many foes, some open, and some disguised; and you may find
friends upon your way when you least look for it" (I, 360): a
fair statement of the moral subtlety which Tolkien has often
been wrongly denied.

Eyed by sinister birds and beset by preternatural wolves whose
carcasses vanish,[25] the company tries to cross the Misty Mountains; but Mount Caradhras attacks them with a blizzard, a
scene Tolkien had saved in his mind since a holiday in the Swiss
Alps when he was nineteen. Boromir is the chief rescuer of the
little hobbits, using his strength patiently to fill their needs.

Foiled above ground, they decide to pass under the mountains
through the mines of Moria, a name of menace since *The Hobbit*.
Gimli alone feels happy to go there, but sorrowful when they find
the disastrous chronicle of a recolonizing party of dwarves. The
Ring-company is shadowed by footsteps, attacked by orcs and
trolls, and, on the verge of escaping, confronted with a balrog.
What a balrog might be, Tolkien's readers had no idea, but even
Gandalf was dismayed. (*The Silmarillion* clarifies their nature:
fiery fallen maiar.) The wizard and his foe plunge into an abyss.

Bruised by his loss, the survivors follow Aragorn to Loth-
lorien, an elf-hold ruled by Galadriel, the Noldorin princess who
had joined the pursuit of Morgoth. She may not return to the
Undying Lands; weary in Middle-earth, she makes her realm as
fair as possible, by the power of her elf-ring. Her gaze tests the
loyalty of each companion; we are reminded that embarrassment
and guilt are not directly proportional.

Gimli has been resenting elves; but Galadriel shows she under-
stands his love of ill-fated Moria:

"Do not repent of your welcome to the Dwarf. . . . Dark is the water
of Kheled-zâram, and cold are the springs of Kibil-nâla, and fair were
the many-pillared halls of Khazad-dûm in Elder Days. . . ." She looked
upon Gimli, who sat glowering and sad, and she smiled. And the
Dwarf, hearing the names given in his own ancient tongue, looked
up and met her eyes; and it seemed to him that he looked suddenly
into the heart of an enemy and saw there love and understanding.
Wonder came into his face, and then he smiled in answer. (I, 461)

Gimli has come down with an intense and pure case of courtly
love: this kind neither pining nor looking toward marriage, but

simply worshipping goodness and beauty when they strike him.[26] Tolkien characteristically has language be the vehicle of this joyful revelation. For his narrative, the principal result is Gimli's now being open to appreciate all good elvish things, especially his companion Legolas. Legolas in turn, touched by Gimli's appreciation, conceives a like friendship for him. Their personal amity helps warm up their previously estranged peoples. The legend that Gimli may have gone over sea to Elvenhome is even more remarkable when one knows what *The Silmarillion* tells about the apartness of the dwarf-race.

Galadriel shows Frodo and Sam visions, all disquieting: the Shire seems to be polluted. Tolkien, ten years before the public consciousness-raising of *Silent Spring*, saw with distress the fragility of ecosystems and the propensity of human beings to commit countrycide.

Frodo sees the searching eye of Sauron, which the queen too senses: "I perceive the Dark Lord and know his mind. . . . And he gropes ever to see me and my thought. But still the door is closed" (I, 472). Here is the advantage of the good side: they can imagine Sauron's thought. Those who reject the Ring can imagine themselves as Saurons. But he is unable to imagine them; the idea of destroying the Ring never enters his mind. Galadriel too rejects the offer of the Ring, and this firmness chiefly causes the Valar to lift their ban against her return to the West.

Leaving Lorien, the company reaches a point of choice: to Mordor with the Ring to the Cracks of Doom, or to Minas Tirith to fight against Sauron? Boromir claims a better idea: take the Ring to Minas Tirith; then the fight will surely succeed. He becomes so possessed with the thought as to attack Frodo, even as he cries, "True-hearted Men, they will not be corrupted" (I, 515). Actually men seem to be the *most* susceptible Ring-victims; no Ring-wielding elf nor dwarf has become Sauron's like the Ring-wraiths. Frodo's only means of escape is invisibility.

Boromir repents soon, and expiates his attack on a hobbit by giving his life for two others; for orcs carry off Merry and Pippin despite his defense. Boromir is an authentic good guy and an authentic bad guy. His bad deeds spring from a seemingly irreproachable source: love of country and well-founded pride in his and his people's achievements. Yet his perspective is distorted: in his grand way, the heir-apparent of Gondor is provincial, like the hobbits in their Shire—and he has more ambition and scope for his provincialism to be dangerous.

Frodo, wearing the Ring, dashes in panic to the Seat of Seeing. There the eye in the Dark Tower almost finds him; but some Voice calls in his mind, "Take off the Ring!" Neither he nor the reader can know it is Gandalf. "Suddenly he was aware of himself again. Frodo, neither the Voice nor the Eye: free to choose. . . . He took the Ring off his finger" (I, 519). Because of Tolkien's beliefs, the free will of his characters is vital to the story.[27] Clear in his mind, Frodo sets off alone for Mordor, joined in the nick of time by Sam.

As book 3, "The Treason of Isengard," begins, the fellowship is scattered. Boromir's body is laid in a boat floating southward;[28] Frodo and Sam are working east over rocky hills; Merry and Pippin are borne westward by orcs; and Aragorn, Legolas, and Gimli are tracking the last party across Rohan, land of the horse-lords. Here begins Tolkien's most striking use of the medieval narrative technique of interlace.[29] As this study strives more for clarity than for suspense, the order of events in this book differs now and then from Tolkien's.

Groups of orcs from the Misty Mountains, Isengard, and Mordor fight each other, showing a spirit like C. S. Lewis's Belbury (in *That Hideous Strength*). Making for Saruman's hold, they are killed by a troop of horsemen under Eomer.

The riders meet the trackers with mutual suspicion. The dwarf, like a true lover, is quite ready to ax a towering man for a slight to the Lady Galadriel. But Aragorn's self-assurance, firmness, and courtesy preserve the peace. Rohan desires "only to be free, and to live as we have lived, keeping our own, and serving no foreign lord, good or evil" (II, 43). But Aragorn, like wartime itself, brings "the doom of choice" (II, 44). Eomer chooses to leave them free, and even lends horses.

But that night a silent old man appears, the horses run off, and the trackers are stranded under the eaves of the menacing Forest of Fangorn (qualm). An even worse qualm awaits them and the reader when next they meet an old man: surely Saruman! But it is *Gandalf*, alive again and dressed in white, taking the position and color vacated by Saruman.

Tolkien, often though not always, does use brightness and darkness symbolically for good and evil.[30] Gandalf's resurrection as the White seems a downright blatant use of such symbolism. But close reading reveals it as consistent with Tolkien's natural history: when the body of a maia gets killed, its next body illustrates more about its character. Thus Sauron, while in Numenor, looked attractive; but after the sinking, he could only appear foul; after that body's defeat, he cannot concoct much semblance at all: an eye, a cloudy shape with nine fingers. Gandalf is undergoing the same process to the opposite end: after being killed by the balrog, he can scarcely keep his light under a bushel or a grey cloak. Each maia undergoes changes such as Paul Valéry refers to: "Tel qu'en lui-même enfin l'éternité le change" ("As eternity at last transforms him into himself").

The wizard gives news of "a house divided against itself": Sauron "'has failed—so far. Thanks to Saruman.' 'Then is not Saruman a traitor?' said Gimli. 'Indeed yes.... Doubly.... [B]etween them our enemies have contrived only to bring Merry and Pippin . . . in the nick of time, to Fangorn!'" (II, 128).

Merry and Pippin, using wits and stamina where they have no strength, have survived and escaped. Pippin, usually the irresponsible hobbit, acquits himself outstandingly; his prankish disposition, often a nuisance, now is a weapon: he deceives a greedy orc by implying that the hobbits could and would help him to the Ring. Loose in Fangorn Wood, Pippin and Merry stand by an old stump wondering what to do.

The stump hails them (qualm). It is Fangorn himself, an ent. "Almost felt you liked the Forest! That's good! That's uncommonly kind of you.... I almost feel that I dislike you both, but do not let us be hasty. . . . *Hrum, Hoom.* . . . if I had seen you before I heard you, I should have just trodden on you, taking you for little orcs" (II, 83–84). Fangorn's voice is the voice of Jack Lewis.[31] Once again, characters are mystified at first and maybe put off by each other. Ents and hobbits have never heard of each other.[32]

Neither had the Rohirrim heard of hobbits except as legends (II, 45). Tolkien repeatedly portrays ignorance with more or less prejudice; even well-disposed human beings have trouble taking hobbits seriously, because of their childlike size. Fangorn utters the only sensible answer to ignorance and prejudice: "do

not let us be hasty." Their qualms changed to nascent liking, he
carries Merry and Pippin home and refreshes them.[33]

With ents, those unrealistic creatures, Tolkien gets to a subject dear to realistic writers: degenerated relations between the
sexes. Ents and entwives had different dispositions, and each sex
followed its own likings, with the upshot that now they do not
know where each other are.[34] Strindberg can separate characters
with more venom and noise, but with no more sadness or plausi-
bility. Ronald and Edith Tolkien's tastes and ways did not mesh
in many areas, and possibly at times they had the feeling of
missing each other even under the same roof.

Fangorn, hearing the hobbits' news, concludes the time has
come to stop tolerating Saruman and his ax-wielding henchfolk:
the ents march to war on Isengard. When Tolkien had studied
Macbeth in school and read of "great Birnham Wood to high
Dunsinane Hill" coming against him, he was thrilled with the
idea, then disgusted with the cheap use Shakespeare made of it.
Human beings with a branch—hah! He resolved to redress the
balance in favor of the Wood.[35] Isengard falls and Saruman
alone remains marooned, for his forces are off fighting Rohan.

Readers have met the lord of Rohan. Gandalf and his companions found an aged, dispirited king, Theoden (Old English,
"Lord of the people"), attended by his niece Eowyn and a
fawning counselor, Grima son of Galmod (Mask son of Lechery).
Gandalf is coldly welcomed, though he urges that "the laughter
of Mordor will be our only reward, if we quarrel" (II, 147). He
unmasks Grima Wormtongue as an agent of Saruman, and Theoden gradually drops his valetudinarian airs. Eowyn feels attracted to the "tall heir of kings," Aragorn (II, 152). Tolkien
thought of marrying them, but decided on a different fate for
each (West, "Variorum").

Tolkien's fiction has been accused of having "no women";
indeed, the modesty and chastity of his writing have caused
deep discomfort to critics reared in the realistic or naturalistic
tradition and the aftermath of Freud's researches, whose conclusions were widely bastardized as "All Is Sex." (These critics
might have been cheered to know about Turin and Nienor.)
If "no women" means "no Masters and Johnson," he has not;[36]
vital female characters, yes.

Eowyn, in particular, is given virtually a case history, though a reader must pick it out from fragments until the end. Her mother died when she was seven, when she and her brother were adopted by a widower uncle with one son. Thus a male would seem to her the normal thing to be. However, she was not; and Grima "son of lechery" took note of her beauty as she grew up: "Too long have you watched her under your eyelids and haunted her steps" (II, 159). Such a reaction from such a person can make a young woman feel downright dirty.

The society of Rohan glorifies horse*men*; and remaining at home would be hard enough for the princess without Grima and his relaying of Saruman's propaganda: "What is the House of Eorl but a thatched barn where brigands drink in the reek, and their brats roll on the floor among the dogs?" (II, 237). Uncomfortable in herself, apparently without female friends, dogged by Grima, watching her dear uncle wither and her dear brother ride off on patrol, she freezes—and no wonder—at a stage most women have passed by her age of twenty-four. Her very name, if translated "joy in horses," hints at an adolescent rather than an adult female.

As Marion Zimmer Bradley remarks, Aragorn's attractiveness to Eowyn is not really that she would like to marry him: she would rather *be* him.[37] Then he too rides off, apparently to his doom, without her. The stage is set for female psychopathology. Ophelia went mad. Does Edith's husband and Priscilla's father condemn or belittle Eowyn, or even simply rescue her? He does not. Recognizing her state as unhealthy, he shows her using her very illness to achieve one of the best ends in the story, as will be seen. Meanwhile in book 3, appointed viceroy explicitly because "She is fearless and high-hearted. All love her" (II, 162), Eowyn feels woefully belittled.

Grima heads for Isengard, unaware of its ruin. Theoden leads his troops to man the stronghold of Helm's Deep, beset by Saruman's host with explosives. The Isengarders are defeated at last by the Rohirrim and—a forest which was not there before. The ents and their herds finish their work: not an orc gets through. But the human survivors are forgiven and set to work, contrary to Saruman's propaganda. This will be another echo of Tolkien's war experience: the prisoner of war surprised that he is not in the hands of monsters.

In the caves behind the fort Gimli has found sights to send him lyrical; but Legolas is fascinated by the forest. Each friend thinks the other "strange folk," but agrees to visit the place the other loves (II, 120, 173, 195). The ents and entwives could have used such charity.

While Rohan musters to go help Gondor, the chief characters ride to Isengard, where they find amid the debris Merry and Pippin smoking pipes; joyful reunion and exchange of news. This episode has been called cloyingly cozy; but C. S. Lewis has remarked on its fidelity to their generation's experiences in World War I: the little island of relaxation and plenty in the devastated landscape.

Saruman, stripped of all but his voice, is Tolkien's picture of the master-propagandist—of which several examples flourished while he was writing. Saruman's eloquent wooing is rejected, and he too rejects Gandalf's invitation to turn again and oppose Sauron (again, a choice offered). A crystal globe hurtles from the tower; Pippin picks it up. Saruman and Grima are locked up alone together: as cozy a Hell as Sartre could devise.

The globe exerts such a fascination that Pippin steals it to gaze into. It is a seeing-stone, a palantir from Elvenhome, and through it Sauron's mind grasps at the hobbit's. Again, ill over-reaches itself: the prey is tougher than the Dark Lord knew, and Sauron lets the contact be broken, jumping to the conclusion that Pippin is (1) the Ring-bearer and (2) at Isengard. Thus his attention is providentially drawn west, reducing the danger to Frodo and Sam headed east on his very borders. Pippin, learning about the palantiri, says, "I had no notion of what I was doing." Gandalf retorts with practical morality: "Oh yes, you had. You knew you were behaving wrongly and foolishly" (II, 260). Book 3 ends with wizard and hobbit galloping toward Minas Tirith.

Book 4, "The Journey of the Ring-bearers," returns to Frodo and Sam and a third traveler: Gollum. Frodo recalls his conversation with Gandalf and admits, "now that I see him, I do pity him" (II, 281). In the face of Sam's disgust and wrath, with the quiet self-assurance of a hero, Frodo takes the abject creature as their guide, bound by the oath "I will serve the master of the Precious" (II, 285).

As the Bearer exacts the oath, Sam sees them as "a mighty lord who hid his brightness in grey cloud, and at his feet a little whining dog. Yet the two were in some way akin and not alien: they could reach one another's minds" (II, 285). Sam, as yet untainted with any trace of Ring-disease, is the odd man out, which preys on him increasingly. Ring-innocence is good, of course; but a person feeling left out easily becomes ashamed even of a virtue.

Tolkien makes vivid the places they traverse; but even more dramatic are the relations of the three characters.[38] Gollum, after his long life with the Ring and his torture in Mordor, has become mad (not stupid). He speaks as two persons: one hissing, cringing "we" and one "I," more coherent and with more backbone. Both are unattractive—especially to Sam. Sam's qualities have been coming out throughout the story, and without question he is an excellent hobbit, Frodo's "dearest hobbit, friend of friends" (II, 292). To have the repulsive, treacherous Gollum promoted to what looks like a similar position is more than the faithful Sam can bear: he is jealous. But when finally his chance comes to kill Gollum, he lets him free: Sam is a merciful person, and by then he too has felt his form of the Ring's temptation (II, 216). But before that, Tolkien ties us a moral Gordian knot.

Shadowed by every kind of menace, Sam says he will watch while Frodo sleeps. But

so Gollum found them hours later . . . Sam . . . his head dropping sideways and his breathing heavy. In his lap lay Frodo's head, drowned deep in sleep. . . . Gollum looked at them. . . . pain seemed to twist him . . . engaged in some interior debate. . . . he touched Frodo's knee— but almost the touch was a caress. For a fleeting moment, [he looked like] an old weary hobbit. . . . [But Sam wakes.] The first thing he saw was Gollum—"pawing at master," as he thought.

"Hey you!" he said roughly. "What are you up to?" . . . Gollum withdrew himself. . . . The fleeting moment had passed, beyond recall. (II, 411)

After reading this climax in the relations of Frodo, Sam, and Gollum, who will still presume to label "good guys" and "bad

guys"? Sam, who has been considered the "best" character in
the story, commits the most tragic deed in the story, killing the
very last kind impulse possible to the ruined Gollum. After that,
Gollum debates and chooses no more, but only presses ahead
in his Ring-madness. Sam's action helps bring Frodo nearer to
death than any minion of Mordor can. Yet in the end, when
Gollum has reached bottom and tries to throw Frodo into the
fire, this undoubtedly "bad" character performs the most vital
good deed in the story: the destruction of the Ring. "But for
him, . . . the Quest would have been in vain. . . . So let us for-
give him! For the Quest is achieved" (III, 277).

For Frodo, after all his toughness, his patience, his heroism,
suddenly has his will wear through. On the brink of the Crack,
which he could never have reached without Sam, he claims the
Ring and could never relinquish it without Gollum. Frodo becomes yet another of Tolkien's hand-marked characters, nine-
fingered like Sauron.[39] We can regard his injury, like Sir Gawain's green baldric, as the sign of both honor and shame.

Frodo, Sam, and Gollum show that while Tolkien often uses
bold contrasts in portraying the moral sphere outside the individual, his picture of the "interior forum" (as churchmen call
one's mind and conscience) is shaded with great subtlety. Those
who call his morality black-and-white ignore his salient love
of grey, which metaphorically extends to the moral sphere.[40]

Before entering Mordor, the travelers are waylaid by some
Robin Hood types, Rangers under Faramir, Boromir's brother.
Tolkien had not expected him. Witnessing their fight with a
Mordor-bound company and looking at a corpse makes Sam
think like Hardy's young soldier:

> Yes, quaint and curious war is:
> You shoot a fellow down
> You'd treat, if met where any bar is,
> Or help to half-a-crown.
>
> ("The Man He Killed")

Again Tolkien refuses to show the dashing aspect of combat
as its only one. He poises, falling into neither romanticism nor
naturalism.

As the oliphaunt charges through, a Ranger cries, "May the Valar turn him aside!" (II, 341). This is a prayer, though one would not recognize it without Tolkien's mythological background. The people of Gondor also have a custom like religious uses in the primary world: "Before they ate, . . . all . . . turned and faced west in a moment of silence." Faramir explains, "we look towards Numenor that was, and beyond Elvenhome that is, and to that which is beyond Elvenhome and will ever be" (II, 361). The Third Age could have no Torah scrolls or crosses, but human beings' impulse to recognize the Providential governance of the world was active from the beginning.

Fatigue and unaccustomed alcohol so tell on Sam that at last he blurts out "Ring" (II, 366). Faramir, like Gandalf, Aragorn, and Galadriel, has his chance to seize it from his "little guests" (II, 367). But learned in the same lore that made them careful, and having pledged his word not to take it, Faramir protects hobbits and Ring. He is an ideal hero of Tolkien's, skilled in war if a war is going on, but inclined to the arts of peace. His two-fold capability is the reason he can win Eowyn: she can easily admire the warrior in him, and then find out how lovable is the peace-lover.

As Mordor sends out an army toward Minas Tirith, Frodo heads inward over Cirith Ungol ("Spider Pass"). Gollum, unable to repent his treachery after Sam's roughness, leads them to Shelob, "last child of Ungoliant," mother of the Mirkwood spiders (II, 423). The hobbits daunt her with a glass holding light from Earendil; and Frodo quotes Cynewulf in Quenya.[41] However, she poisons Frodo.

Despair attacks Sam, and thoughts of vengeance and suicide; at last he realizes the Ring must be borne forward. He takes it and, as orcs approach, puts it on: probably the only character who could do so on the verge of Mordor, since he has never borne it, and his mind never become attuned to it; and his motive is completely altruistic. Even so, he feels not invisible but exposed.

The orcs reveal that Frodo is still alive! He is carried into their tower and Sam is locked out. Here volume 2 ends. Sir Stanley Unwin's mailbox filled with expressions of panic. Paperback readers have been known to rush into the streets at 2:00

A.M. in search of an all-night bookstore. Frodo and Sam's story continues in book 6, "The End of the Third Age."

Seeing Shelob has been hurt, the orcs deduce a great elvish warrior; and for his master, Sam Gamgee will play even that role: the orc saw "not a small frightened hobbit trying to hold a steady sword: it saw a great silent shape, cloaked in shadow . . . ; in one hand it held a sword, the very light of which was a bitter pain, the other was clutched at its breast, but held concealed some nameless menace of power and doom" (III, 220). Sam need hardly fight, since the orcs with characteristic charm have massacred each other, quarreling over Frodo's mithril-mail.

Sam rescues Frodo. We see the Ring's eroding of Frodo's mind when he grabs it back, calling Sam "thief" (III, 230). Disguised in orc-gear, they set forth into Mordor itself; Fangorn's impression of Merry and Pippin ("little orcs") shows the disguise is not too farfetched, especially as orcs do come in various conformations.

Meanwhile book 5, "The War of the Ring," returns to Gandalf and Pippin arriving at Minas Tirith. Denethor, the ruling Steward, sits before the empty throne mourning his son Boromir. Pippin feels "pride [stir] strangely within him, still stung by the scorn and suspicion in that cold voice" (III, 30), and swears fealty to Denethor. Between him and Gandalf, Pippin senses tension. "Denethor looked indeed much more like a great wizard . . . , more kingly, beautiful, and powerful; and older. Yet . . . Gandalf had the greater power and the deeper wisdom, and a majesty that was veiled. And he was older" (III, 32). In fact, the wizards have been in Middle-earth some two thousand years.

Gandalf reminds the lord of Gondor: "the rule of no realm is mine. . . . But all worthy things that are in peril . . . are my care. . . . I shall not wholly fail . . . though Gondor should perish, if anything passes through this night that can still grow fair or bear fruit and flower again. . . . For I also am a steward. Did you not know?" (III, 33–34). That is what the wizards are for, what Saruman failed at, and what the human steward Denethor in his degree is finally failing at too. Tolkien's concern with responsible stewardship fits well with his concern for ecology.

As Pippin is shown the forces of Gondor marching into the city, Tolkien lets himself go for once in an epic catalog, though mostly in *The Lord of the Rings* he has shorn such material out of the main text and put it into the appendices.[42] His verve and wealth of names makes one forget that Tolkien is inventing it all, not recording.

Faramir returns, to be reproached by Denethor for not bringing him "a mighty gift" (III, 104). The Steward seems surprisingly well informed. He openly flouts Gandalf, denying that the Ring would burn his mind away. As it turns out, a lesser object has done so. Denethor's knowledge and apparent wisdom are explained three chapters later when we learn that Minas Tirith has a palantir. The Steward does not realize that everything he has seen, while true in itself, has been edited by Sauron to drive him to despair.

Sauron acts in haste, because Aragorn has wrenched the palantir of Isengard to his own will. Sauron, thinking he sees a new Ring-lord, throws an army under Angmar against Minas Tirith before Aragorn can get there. Faramir takes a poisoned arrow. All Gondor awaits their allies of Rohan.

Meanwhile Rohan has mustered. Merry swears fealty to the gracious Theoden, as Pippin did to Denethor, but out of love rather than pride. Merry too has a deed to do. Aragorn heads southward to confront a corsair fleet whose nearness has kept many from the defense of the city. His shortcut is the Paths of the Dead.

Tolkien knows—it is a major point in *The Silmarillion*—that the fate of dead human beings is not in this world. He is also confronted with stories everywhere of dead people active in the world: from the spirit of Samuel conjured in the Bible (1 Samuel 28) to the dumb warriors revived by the cauldron in *The Mabinogion*, i.e., either soul or body working without the other. Chief of Mordor's fighters are its wraiths of dread. Tolkien answers them—Gimli notes the irony (III, 186)—with an army of human ghosts, normal men who broke an oath to fight against Sauron and have waited over three thousand years for the occasion to do so and be released. Their special Purgatory was in Middle-earth.

Tolkien repeatedly uses pairs: "ghost" in itself is not good or bad, for he shows us both; the same for "wizard," "tree-man," "maia," and for that matter, "man."

The oathbreakers rout the corsairs, in whose ships Aragorn

sets sail for Minas Tirith. The wind changes to help him, as it did for Joan of Arc before Orléans.

Theoden and his army avoid orcs with the help of aborigines doubtless adapted from Tolkien's own juvenile adventure reading: hunters and trackers with a dignity of their own, whom "civilized" people have harried unjustly. Squire Merry was to be left behind, but rides under the cloak of the young soldier Dernhelm (Old English, "Helm of Secrecy"). Rohan's horns announce their arrival as Minas Tirith nears despair.

Within, Denethor "has fallen before his city is taken" (III, 123). Anxious and remorseful over Faramir and misled by his palantir, the great Steward plunges into despair. Despair, there is a strong guess among theologians, is the one unforgivable sin (Matthew 12:31–32), because it denies God's love, power or both, whereas really both are infinite.

Denethor presents as extreme a case of this state as Marlowe's Doctor Faustus. He orders himself and Faramir burned. Pippin flies for Gandalf, who is just confronting Angmar. At the horns of Rohan, the wraith draws off like a ghost at cock-crow, and Gandalf hastens to Denethor. Again, every chance of rescue is given a character who can choose; but Denethor repudiates all. Though he boasts of having kept in training (III, 111), he will not advance a foot to do the least helpful deed; by contrast to Theoden, who has thrown off his dotage and is leading his cavalry outside. Denethor, like the Greek Aegeus, has seen black sails approaching and "knows" all is lost. When Gandalf mentions the possible coming of the King, the Steward says he will have rule or *naught* (III, 158), thus destroying all he has kept for so long, pulling himself out by the roots. He ignites his pyre and burns to death like a heathen (III, 157)—another of Tolkien's rare religious terms.

Out on the field, epic battles are waged. Theoden is attacked by Angmar, the wraith secure in an ancient prophecy that "not by the hand of man shall he fall" (III, 412). Like Macbeth's "none of woman born," it was a trick: Angmar finds himself withstood by a woman and a hobbit. Dernhelm was Eowyn, seeking a warrior's death: using her personal despair to at least help her uncle and her country.

The process of Angmar's defeat has raised questions as to where the credit lies; the final driving of the wraith from earthly appearance goes like this: Merry's barrow-blade hamstrings the wraith as it would an ordinary solid body; most weapons would not.[43] Angmar naturally stumbles forward, stooping his head into range of Eowyn's stroke. Though the head is invisible, her blade's shattering proves it has struck, and at that point the wraith must flee its clothing and its existence in Middle-earth.

Merry and Eowyn are more severely hurt by his being than by bodily injuries: both suffer from the Black Breath. Only the King can heal them and the exhausted, fevered Faramir.

Aragorn will not take up the kingship at such a confused time; but to heal, he will enter the city incognito. Some ado has been made about his healing as parallel to Christ's.[44] Tolkien, in praising Aragorn, emphasizes his descent from Luthien (III, 264); we know this is a compliment to Edith, whom her husband considered to come of the same unfailing line.

The allies, knowing they "must at all costs keep [Sauron's] Eye from his true peril" (III, 191), feint with an army to the gate of Mordor. There Sauron's herald urges them to despair by producing Frodo's mail; and an unequal battle is joined. Again the eagles arrive. At that moment Mordor quakes and its forces lose heart; for the Ring is in the fire.

Frodo and Sam, shadowed by Gollum, have made their way across the foul land. Sam thinks of the Shire and Rosie Cotton.[45] We hear plenty about homesickness on Tolkien's journeys, but this is the first we have heard of a girl; as in *The Song of Roland*, where Aude is not mentioned until a crisis in battle. "But even as hope died in Sam, or seemed to die, it was turned to a new strength" (III, 259); he too develops Maldon-syndrome, will the sterner as his might lessens. Tempted to lie down and sleep, he instead takes charge and even carries Frodo, whose mind is nearly sapped.

"No taste of food, no feel of water, no sound of wind, no memory of tree or grass or flower, no image of moon or star are left to me. I am naked in the dark, Sam, and there is no veil between me and the wheel of fire. I begin to see it even with my waking eyes, and all else fades." (III, 264)

On Mount Doom occur Sam's repudiation of his long-awaited chance to kill Gollum, Frodo's claiming of the Ring, and Gollum's fall with it into the fire. Mordor crumbles; Sauron is unbodied again. The two survivors are rescued by eagles and Gandalf, whom they had thought dead. "Is everything sad going to come untrue?" gasps Sam (III, 283).

Tolkien sets all in order. Because of the destruction of the Ring, Gondor will now begin its year on March twenty-fifth, as was done in England until 1751. The year began in spring, on Lady Day, the feast of the Annunciation, when Mary said "Yes" to having a baby and redemption began for humankind.

Tolkien lets his love of splendor and ceremony flow free and reverses all the signs of woe round Gondor. Aragorn is crowned; women and children return to Minas Tirith, now properly renamed Minas Anor (Tower of the Sun instead of Tower of Guard); dwarves plan to restore its stonework and elves its gardens; a seedling is found to replace the dead Tree; and Arwen comes to marry the King.

The companions retrace their journey, giving gifts and tying up loose ends. At Isengard no prisoner remains: Saruman has talked Fangorn into letting him and Grima go. The travelers meet them, and once more Gandalf extends a choice to Saruman, who rejects it. Wormtongue whines, "'How I hate him! I wish I could leave him!' 'Then leave him!' said Gandalf" (III, 324). But Grima, like someone in Lewis's *Great Divorce*, only looks terrified and skulks off in his master's wake. He will not be free, he will not be bound; in the end, all he does is kill.

As *The Hobbit* was not over with Smaug's death and the Battle of the Five Armies, since Bilbo's home was imperilled, so *The Lord of the Rings* returns to ills in the Shire. Gandalf tells the four hobbits, "You must settle its affairs yourselves; that is what you have been trained for.... You are grown up now ... among the great you are, and I have no longer any fear for any of you" (III, 340). The War of the Ring as training for the Scouring of the Shire! There is Tolkien's perspective on the importance of the Great World and of Home.

The returning hobbits find jerry-built barracks, regimentation, pollution, no tobacco, and no beer: a scene like Lewis's Edgestow under the N.I.C.E. *(That Hideous Strength)*, or such as England could easily imagine under victorious Nazis. The acquisitive Sackville-Bagginses, like Lewis's Curry, have invited something bigger and worse than they know into their good land. Gaining a foothold through commerce, Saruman has holed up here, with human and hobbit bullies in the ascendant.

The travelers are sad, angry, and of course no whit daunted; the local hobbitry needs only their leadership to raise an unpretentious, effective revolution. We see that the revolution Tolkien respects is not ideological, but a concrete matter of how one is to live. If you cannot gather in a pub for a beer with friends, your government needs changing. The four hobbits divide the royal qualities which Aragorn unites. Merry takes command; he and Pippin lead battles—" 'Lordly,' folk called them, meaning nothing but good" (III, 377); Frodo insists on mercy; Sam holds office, restores vegetation, marries, and has a family.

Saruman and Grima are given yet another chance. At last the worm turns (Tolkien playing with clichés again) and Grima stabs his master, who dissolves in smoke as Sauron did. The tyrant master has denatured his servant and formed his own doom; Frodo has led his servant to be a hero.[46]

Frodo "dropped quietly out of all the doings of the Shire" (III, 377), sickening on the anniversaries of his wounds. He cannot stay: the Shire "has been saved, but not for me. It must often be so, Sam, when things are in danger: someone has to give them up, lose them, so that others may keep them" (III, 382). His quest has succeeded in losing the Ring, in losing Gollum, and in losing his everyday life. As in book 1, he leaves Bag End and meets elves in the woods. This time they ride west, to the Grey Havens, whence the Ring-bearers will be carried off the globe by a straight road to the West, as Frodo saw in a dream at Bombadil's.

The book does not end with the story, for Tolkien gives us six appendices with languages, calendars, and history.[47] Small wonder Allen and Unwin were daunted. Tolkien himself was surprised (happily) to learn from letters that admirers found the books "too short" (I, x).

The Lord of the Rings will continue to be widely read only if people like reading it. Whether they do or not, the work deserves respect for the rigor with which Tolkien has followed every lead of his material. Seldom has a setting been more solidly built or thoroughly explored.[48] Argument can see-saw as to whether Tolkien's greatest merit is his inventiveness or his values.

For his last twenty years, he could speak of the three volumes as Yavanna spoke of the Two Trees and Fëanor of the three Silmarils: "Even for those who are mightiest under Ilúvatar there is some work that they may accomplish once, and once only. . . . never again shall I make their like" (S, 78).

CHAPTER 7

Fantasy and Realism: Sadness and Hope

That noble Extravagance of Fancy, which he had in so great Perfection . . . made him capable of succeeding, where he had nothing to support him besides the Strength of his own Genius. There is something . . . in the Speeches of his Ghosts, Fairies, Witches and the like Imaginary Persons, that we cannot forbear thinking them natural, though we have no Rule by which to judge of them, and must confess, if there are such Beings in the World, it looks highly probable they should talk and act as he has represented them.

Joseph Addison, *Spectator Papers*, 419

TOLKIEN'S imagination or his values: which is the more important aspect of his writing? Neither. Both. The two are not separate. Studying his thought and his art, we can see them meet in his treatment of material creation, the "primary world." We find continuity among Tolkien and much literature from the past (chapter 2, sections I–III), but a sharp discontinuity with the art and philosophy prevailing in his hemisphere during the decades of his adulthood (section IV).

The master of fantasy is the master of realism. This seeming paradox is clear in painting: take a rectangle by Mondrian, a blob by Arp, some triangles by Kandinsky, and no one can tell whether the painting be fantasy or not. Viewers can enjoy the colored shapes, but only as themselves, not with reference to an object outside the painting. A grey shape by Tanguy *is* his grey shape, not a picture *of* a piece of driftwood or anything. Such art is properly called nonobjective;[1] it is neither realism nor fantasy.

But take a boulder by Magritte, meticulously rendered; on it stands a castle, meticulously rendered. Boulder and castle float in the air over the sea, also carefully painted. This picture, clearly, is a fantasy, and gains from the realism of its technique.

121

So with Tolkien's writing: his acquaintance with and love of the primary world permeate and strengthen his writings of fantasy. His "noble extravagance of fancy" springs to the eye; yet the more one reads, the more his realism becomes apparent. Caring about all creatures from archangels to stalactites, Tolkien stretched his imagination to embrace them all. Without the discipline of realism, fantasy would be impossible.

This fantasy based on realism differs from both nonobjective art and "Ashcan realism" in painting and literature. The play of subcreation in which the fantasy artist revels shows a relaxed certainty about the primary world which Dadaists and Ashcanists generally lack.[2] Both the certainty and the uncertainty have philosophical connections; whether the personal attitudes are rooted in the philosophies, or the philosophies in the personal feelings of their adherents, one can hardly say.

Tolkien spoke of the pre-Christian setting of *Beowulf* as "heathen, noble, and hopeless." And Tolkien, orphaned and bereft of friends, found himself in a culture where leading thinkers and writers fitted that very description, though their dates read "year of Our Lord." Zamyatin in Russia, Kafka in Austria, Brecht in Germany, the titanic Sartre in France, and scores more were as heathen, noble, and hopeless as any troll-harried Dane, while the years carried them from war through depression into war again. Tolkien could turn in every direction and see a world of strangers, heaving with nausea in a wasteland.[3]

Antoine Roquentin, protagonist of Sartre's *Nausée*, feels he exists like a blob by Arp: unrelated to the primary—let alone any secondary—world.[4] The sadness evident in much twentieth-century literature and philosophy, both exemplified by Sartre, nears despair. Ashcan realism in words or paint has its own desperation: a striving to pin down the primary world, as if it might run away unless the human artist fixed it. One recalls tribes who believed the sun would never return without sacrifices at the solstice.[5]

Tolkien and his characters, despite their various personal sadnesses, remain hopeful; and a major foundation of their hope is simply the reality of the world. Tolkien, like Magritte, can build his fantasies carefully, certain that the material he builds from—"The green earth, say you? That is a mighty matter of legend, though you tread it under the light of day!" (II, 45)— really exists. "Exist" for him, unlike Roquentin, is a comforting word; the "real extra-mental existence" of matter bolsters us. Though we may scrape a knee on granite, we can also contemplate precious stones and imagine the Arkenstone. Pippin's nausea at orcs' meat is less distressing, more wholesome, than Roquentin's nausea of doubting his own beer mug.

So Tolkien's beliefs and his art are visibly related. That he can subcreate a secondary world contradicts the "heathen, noble and hopeless" stance prevalent in his time. He denied that he was up to anything in *The Lord of the Rings* except writing a story (I, ix); but, considering the mind and art of his time, we need not be surprised that his story has been waved as a standard, as well as giving its readers pleasure. One conscientious Jesuit, wondering whether he ought to treat himself to Tolkien's fiction during the serious grief of the Vietnam War, concluded, "These books make it more exciting to walk in the woods."[6]

Though *The Silmarillion*, which Tolkien considered his major work, shows things getting worse and worse, his detailed study of the end of an age and the passing of lovable races is a hopeful work. Superficial readers have found *The Lord of the Rings* facilely hopeful; Kocher more accurately says "*at bottom* a hopeful tale."[7] How can Tolkien hope? The answer within him, of course, cannot be seen; but two answers can be guessed: religion and experience.

Tolkien was acquainted with grief and sensed some menace in the universe which would rob us of all good things.[8] The teachings of Catholicism clarified the menace (fallen angels), but overshadowed them with the magnitude of the Creator's care for us: not only does He will our good, but also He has shared all our pain.[9] And not physical pain alone: the Gospels also show Jesus's grief at the death of a friend, and tradition believes that his family underwent the death of St. Joseph. So in both weal and woe, Tolkien knew himself included in the "communion of saints," the fellowship of God's friends in this world and departed from it.

To boot, it seems that daily life itself forbade Tolkien to despair or to become permanently nauseated. The planet sprouted beauties at him which his mother's training, especially in botany, had prepared him to appreciate.[10] Heated water refreshed his body and hops his heart. And he could not help—however bad the circumstances—meeting human beings who enlivened his hope: Edith; the plodding troops who carried out the fight; the "small hands" who do the "deeds that move the wheels of the world . . . because they must, while the eyes of the great are elsewhere" (I, 353); friends to cover his bare back,[11] with whom he could share the planet's pleasures.

He names his leading human character Hope: Estel was Aragorn's child-name (III, 420). But impressive as this king of men is, Tolkien's hope is concentrated in the figure of the hobbit, that is, every-mere-body.[12] Hobbits are unquenchable in a way that the Dark Lord can never know.

Many of the explanations about Tolkien in this study refer to his beliefs as a Catholic. Yet there are Catholics who shrug at Tolkien's stories, and people devoted to Tolkien's stories who would not willingly touch Catholicism with a barge pole. The latter are easily understood; for Tolkien never preaches, let alone taking a denominational line. The matters his work touches— hope and despair; chance, will, and Providence; heroism; love— are not denominational. Many people of this time would apply Cynewulf's words to Tolkien himself: in our decades the "brightest messenger sent to the men of Middle-earth."

Appendix

I wrote to Professor Tolkien because I was going to give a talk on him and there was little material in print. I asked him whether he had tastes, habits, or characteristics which he would not mind our knowing. He replied as follows:

25 October 1958

Dear Miss Webster,

Thank you for your letter, and the little book of collects, so charmingly decorated. I am sorry you did not call on me in the Summer. I was in Oxford most of the time, since my plans for visiting various countries, including U.S.A., had to be cancelled, owing to my wife's illness. I like seeing people. But I do not like giving "facts" about myself other than "dry" ones (which anyway are quite as relevant to my books as any other more juicy details). Not simply for personal reasons; but also because I object to the contemporary trend in criticism, with its excessive interest in the details of the lives of authors and artists. They only distract attention from an author's works (if the works are in fact worthy of attention), and end, as one now often sees, in becoming the main interest. But only one's guardian Angel, or indeed God Himself, could unravel the real relationship between personal facts and an author's works. Not the author himself (though he knows more than any investigator), and certainly not so-called "psychologists".

But, of course, there's a scale of significance in "facts" of this sort. There are insignificant facts (those particularly dear to analysts and writers about writers): such as drunkenness, wife-beating, and suchlike disorders. I do not happen to be guilty of these particular sins. But if I were, I should not suppose that artistic work proceeded from the weaknesses that produced them, but from other and still uncorrupted regions of my being. Modern "researchers" inform me that Beethoven cheated his publishers, and abominably ill-treated his nephew; but I do not

125

believe that has anything to do with his music. Then there are
more significant facts, which *have* some relation to an author's
works; though knowledge of them does not really explain the
works, even if examined at length. For instance I dislike French,
and prefer Spanish to Italian—but the relation of these facts to
my taste in languages (which is obviously a large ingredient in
The Lord of the Rings) would take a long time to unravel, and
leave you liking (or disliking) the names and bits of language
in my books, just as before. And there are a few basic facts,
which however drily expressed, are really significant. For instance I was born in 1892 and lived for my early years in "the
Shire" in a premechanical age. Or more important, I am a
Christian (which can be deduced from my stories), and in fact
a Roman Catholic. The latter 'fact' perhaps cannot be deduced;
though one critic (by letter) asserted that the invocations of
Elbereth; and the character of Galadriel as directly described
(or through the words of Gimli and Sam) were clearly related
to Catholic devotion to Mary. Another saw in waybread (*lem-
bas*):=viaticum: and the reference to its feeding the *will* (vol.
III, p. 213) and being more potent when fasting, a derivation
from the Eucharist. (That is: far greater things may colour the
mind in dealing with the lesser things of a fairy-story.)

I am in fact a *hobbit* (in all but size). I like gardens, trees
and unmechanized farmlands; I smoke a pipe, and like good
plain food (unrefrigerated), but detest French cooking; I like,
and even dare to wear in these dull days, ornamental waistcoats.
I am fond of mushrooms (out of a field); have a very simple
sense of humor (which even my appreciative critics find tiresome); I go to bed late and get up late (when possible). I do
not travel much. I love Wales (what is left of it, when mines,
and the even more ghastly sea-side resorts, have done their
worst), and especially the Welsh language. But I have not in
fact been in W. for a long time (except for crossing it on the
way to Ireland. I go frequently to Ireland (Eire: Southern Ireland) being fond of it and of (most of) its people; but the Irish
language I find wholly unattractive. I hope that is enough to
go on with.

Yours, with gratitude for appreciation,
J.R.R. Tolkien

Notes and References

Preface

1. When Tolkien wrote *The Hobbit*, the modern fashion in buildings was skyscrapers; but he may yet prove a prophet in architecture, if the expense of heating and cooling boxlike structures makes the insulating property of earth attractive enough. Tolkien might be amused to know that the "Farm of the Future," at the Living History Farms in Des Moines, is to be built largely underground. A hole can be practical as well as snug.

2. Tolkien is credited with the transformation in Lester Del Rey, "A Report on J. R. R. Tolkien," *Worlds of Fantasy*, 1 (October, 1968), 84–85.

3. Comparing Tolkien with Shakespeare is not presumptuous. Both men as they wrote were considered less significant than some of their contemporaries (Maugham, Waugh; Chapman, Jonson). Both wrote from a strong literary tradition, not apparently straining to innovate, yet opening new territory. And both have been imitated since, with partial-to-poor success. Tolkien, though not the first writer of modern fantasy, is its first widely recognized master.

4. Letter to Deborah Webster, printed in full in appendix.

5. Wholesale Freudianism is slashed at by Dorothy Sayers and C. S. Lewis, and notably debunked in Frederick C. Crews, *The Pooh Perplex* (mock-scholarly essays); and Charlotte Armstrong, *A Dram of Poison* (suspense novel).

6. Walter Scheps, "The Fairy-tale Morality of *The Lord of the Rings*," in *A Tolkien Compass*, ed. Jared Lobdell (La Salle, Ill., 1975). A paper on "The Geology of Middle-earth" was given by James B. Orr at the Tolkien conference at Champaign-Urbana, Spring 1969. Orr finds the geology satisfyingly comprehensible in terms of the primary world, with three exceptions, each considered special within the tale too: the Lonely Mountain (a maverick volcano, Orr believes); the Arkenstone (most probably a zircon formed in its slowest-cooling part); and mithril (some natural alloy, very likely including silver and platinum). Cf. Margaret Howes, "The Elder Ages and the Later Glaciations of the Pleistocene Epoch," *Tolkien Journal*, 3, no. 2 (1967). (I think *The Silmarillion* supersedes this.)

7. In *The Tolkien Reader* (New York, 1966). Secondary World quotation, p. 37; hereafter cited in text as *TR*.

8. The word worship comes from the same root as worth, and means honor in due measure, not idolatry. Once a scholar had heard someone give a paper on Shire coinage, about which Tolkien says nothing, so the paper was speculation. The scholar, looking bewildered, asked me, "What is he *doing*?" I answered something about playing (speculating) within the secondary world because one loves Tolkien's story. The scholar's brow cleared and with a beautiful look of understanding he said, "Oh! You mean it's an act of worship."

9. Erich Leinsdorff said this on the radio, paraphrasing a book he had read about Mozart.

Chapter One

1. The Birmingham Oratory had been founded in 1849 by John Henry Newman, a famous (or notorious, depending on the point of view) and learned convert from Anglicanism to Roman Catholicism.

2. Bunter, Dorothy Sayers's batman-turned-valet, is another literary tribute to the uncommon *virtú* of the common man. Cf. *Watership Down*, based on Richard Adams's war experiences.

3. *The Fellowship of the Ring* (New York, 1965), p. 258. Hereafter cited in the text as I; *The Two Towers* as II; *The Return of the King* as III.

4. Humphrey Carpenter, *Tolkien* (Boston, 1977), p. 84.

5. Daniel Grotta-Kurska, *J. R. R. Tolkien, Architect of Middle-Earth* (Philadelphia, 1976), p. 93. The book is not reliable, but this anecdote is plausible. *Si non e vero, e ben trovato.*

6. J. I. M. Stewart said, "He could turn a lecture room into a mead hall in which he was the bard and we were the feasting, listening guests" (Carpenter, p. 133).

7. Cf. C. S. Lewis, *Surprised by Joy* (London, 1959), p. 173.

8. Cf. Tolkien's Valedictory Address of 1959, in *J. R. R. Tolkien, Scholar and Storyteller*, ed. Mary Salu and Robert T. Farrell (Ithaca, 1979), pp. 16–32.

9. Some of Major Lewis's essays have been published under the title of *The Splendid Century* (1953; reprint ed., Garden City, N.Y., 1957). Though Versailles never was Tolkien's cup of tea, he enjoyed Warren Lewis's studies—as anyone would, for they are clear and make their writer's interest contagious.

10. Cf. Humphrey Carpenter, *The Inklings* (Boston, 1979), passim.

11. In his introduction to Williams's *All Hallows' Eve* (New York, 1969), p. xi.

12. *The Four Loves* (New York, 1960), p. 92.

13. Letter to Charles Moorman, quoted in Richard C. West, "Tolkien in the Letters of C. S. Lewis," *Orcrist*, I, 13 (p. 11 in fourth reprint).

14. Grotta-Kurska, p. 96.

15. Ibid., p. 112.

16. Tolkien could not stomach the Narnia chronicles, produced at a brisk pace while he was laboring over *The Lord of the Rings*. "It really won't do! I mean to say: 'Nymphs and their Ways, The Love-Life of a Faun'!" (Carpenter, p. 201).

Chapter Two

1. Cf. Joseph Campbell, *Masks of God: Creative Mythology* (New York, 1968); Anne C. Petty, *One Ring to Bind Them All* (University, Ala., 1979).

2. The use of "myth" to mean false is a common debased usage. The word which implies "good story but not factual" is *legend*. Mythologies include legendary material among their stories; legends often crystallize round factual characters.

3. Carpenter, pp. 89–90.

4. On the identity of the Incarnate, see John 1: "Verbum erat apud Deum, et Deus erat Verbum. . . . Omnia per ipsum facta sunt, et sine ipso factum est nihil, quod factum est. . . . Et Verbum caro factum est et habitavit in nobis" ("The Word was with God, and the Word was God. All things were made through him, and without him nothing was made which has come to be. And the Word was made flesh, and dwelt among us").

5. En passant par la Lorraine avec mes sabots; "Rencontrai trois capitaines; / Ils m'ont appelée vilaine; / Je ne suis pas si vilaine, / Si le Fils du Roi m'aime!"

6. *The Adventures of Tom Bombadil* (London, 1962), p. 53. Hereafter cited as *ATB*. Reprinted with same pagination in *A Tolkien Reader* (New York, 1966).

7. Today's Brittany, the peninsula on the French coast; contrasted with Great Britain, the island.

8. E.g., "Those who in the past obeyed the dictates of love were accounted valiant, generous and worthy, but now love is turned into a trifling thing" (Chrétien de Troyes, *Yvain*, ll. 1121ff; Trans. Ackerman, Locke, and Carroll, New York, 1977). Two of the best specimens of the *ubi sunt* ("Where are they now?") theme are the fifteenth-century Villon's two ballades of ladies and lords, with their refrains "Mais où sont les neiges d'antan?" and "Autant en emporte le vent."

9. For this summary I am indebted to Dr. Deborah Jones Webster.

10. Tolkien was not fond of Andersen's tales (Carpenter, p. 22).

11. "No Way Out" and "The Human Condition" are in fact the titles of two notable works of the period: André Malraux' novel of the Chinese Communist revolution *La Condition humaine* (1933) and Jean-Paul Sartre's play *Huis clos* (1944), with its devastating conclusion, "Hell is other people."

12. *Poems* (London, 1964), p. 1.

13. In Samuel Beckett's play *Endgame* (1957).

14. Frye elaborates this scheme beautifully in the first essay of his *Anatomy of Criticism* (Princeton, 1957).

15. Mirlees, *Lud-in-the-Mist* (1926); Eddison, *The Worm Ouroboros* (1926), *Mistress of Mistresses* (1935), *A Fish Dinner in Memison* (1941), *The Mezentian Gate* (1958). These books and several by Dunsany and Cabell, and more, were reprinted in the Ballantine Adult Fantasy series under the editorhip of Lin Carter in the late 1960s. That series was one happy effect of *The Lord of the Rings*; the story descended into Limbo and freed its languishing fellows. For more fantasy of the period, see *Anatomy of Wonder*, ed. Neil Barron (New York, 1976).

Chapter Three

1. Carpenter, p. 45.

2. Ibid., pp. 67f.

3. Richard C. West, "The Interlace and Professor Tolkien," *Orcrist*, I, 31 (reprint ed., p. 22). A revised version of the essay appears in *A Tolkien Compass*, ed. Jared Lobdell (LaSalle, Ill., 1975). An example of Tolkien's carrying on a medieval narrative tradition is his modern Breton lay, "Aotrou and Itroun" ("Lord and Lady" in the Breton language). It stands apart from Tolkien's other writings by the intimacy of its concerns—though his telling is as chaste as ever—and by its tragic outcome; in these respects it resembles many ballads which have preserved old tales over centuries.

Aotrou and Itroun have no children. The Lord finally seeks the help of a witch, unknown to his wife. The corrigan's (Celtic for a woman with second sight, or a witch) charm achieves the conception of twins; but she demands as her price the love of Aotrou. Refusing this payment, he dies, followed by his grieving lady.

Tolkien does not use the ballad stanza nor any form from a stanzaic lay, but octosyllabic couplets: an excellent form for narratives composed to be heard. He uses a sort of refrain as a playwright might use a curtain, varying his opening "In Britain's land beyond the seas" passage. (*Welsh Review*, 4 [December 1943], 254–66.) Cf. *The Breton Lays in Middle English*, ed. Thomas C. Rumble (Detroit, 1965); Marie de France, *Lais*, ed. A. Ewert (Oxford, 1963)—she too uses octosyllabic couplets. An excellent paper on the Breton lay in England was given at the Conference on Medieval Studies at Kalamazoo in May, 1979: Carl Lindahl, "And One of Them Have I in Remembrance: The Franklin's Tale as a Breton Lay." On the "linguistic origin" of Tolkien's stories, see T. A. Shippey, "Creation from Philology," in *J. R. R. Tolkien, Scholar and Storyteller*, ed. Salu and Farrell (Ithaca, 1979), pp. 306ff.

4. J. R. R. Tolkien and Donald Swann, *The Road Goes Ever On* (Boston, 1967), p. 59.

5. Gawain's particular persevering, quiet heroism as he journeys to get his head cut off is saluted in John Myers Myers, *Silverlock* (1949; reprint ed., New York, 1979), an outstanding fantasy.

6. *The Tolkien Reader* (New York, 1966), first p. 10. (The book has four sets of page numbers, as it retains the numbering from the hardcover books.) Gordon's edition of *Maldon* has been reprinted (New York, 1966). Cf. Fred C. Robinson, "God, Death and Loyalty in *The Battle of Maldon*," Salu and Farrell, pp. 76–98.

7. "Tolkien was deeply irritated by this radio production, which ignored the alliterative meter and delivered the verse as if it were iambic pentameters. He himself recorded a version that was much more to his own satisfaction" (Carpenter, p. 214).

8. "The Mewlips" and "The Adventures of Tom Bombadil" (Carpenter, pp. 271, 162). Considering Carpenter's account of Edith Tolkien (p. 155), I wonder whether the dread on the doorstep was her husband's or hers.

9. "The Man in the Moon Stayed up Too Late" (*ATB*, 31 and I, 216ff.) and "The Man in the Moon Came Down Too Soon" (*ATB*, 34). George Burke Johnston points out that George Macdonald combines the same two nursery-rhymes ("The Poetry of J. R. R. Tolkien," *Mankato Studies in English*, 2 (February, 1967). Beatrix Potter shares this urge to embroider on Mother Goose: "Three Little Kittens" is the basis for her *Tale of Tom Kitten*, and "This Little Pig Went to Market" for *Pigling Bland*. Johnston also examines the first version of "The Stone Troll."

10. Lines were named for the number of feet in them; Dr. Webster has written a mnemonic:

DANcing DImeter,	**2 feet**
LIGHTly TRIPping TRImeter;	3

of BETter LENGTH, oft-USED teTRAmeter;   4
a TRIfle SOberER is GRAVE penTAmeter;   5
and an Ocean ROAR like Waves on a SHORE,
    ROLling hexAmeter.   6
These are the lines of verse and song,
the quick and the slow, the short and the long.
Composing *them* are *many feet*:
I*am*bus, *for*ward-*bend*ing, *fleet*;
*Tro*chee, *shy*ly *hold*ing *back*,
*ev*er *lagging on* the *track*.
Like a *cat* that would *spring* seems the A*na*pest *sly*,
crouching *low*, muscles *tense*, with a *keen*, crafty *eye*.
Slow, grim, proud, cold, stalks S*pon*dee; *last*
like *gal*loping *hor*ses the *Dac*tyls flash *past*.

11. Tolkien talks about alliterative verse in his appendixes to his edition and his translation of *Sir Gawain and the Green Knight*, whose author used the old-fashioned form with his Middle English language.

12. "Joyne your hands lovingly: well done, musition! / Mirth keepeth man in health like a phisition . . . / Make a ring on the grasse with your quick measures, / Tom shall play, and Ile sing for all your pleasures" (quoted in Lincoln Kirstein, Introduction, in *A Midsummer Night's Dream* (New York, 1960), p. 26.

13. *Master of Middle-earth*, p. 55.

14. Carpenter, p. 270.

15. *The Young Magicians*, ed. Lin Carter (New York, 1969), p. 259.

16. Cf. *A Medieval Bestiary*, ed. T. J. Elliott (Boston, 1971); T. H. White, *A Book of Beasts* (New York, 1954); David Day et al., *A Tolkien Bestiary* (New York, 1979). C. S. Lewis, with his singing beast in *Perelandra*, is crying for its interpretation in the manner of medieval bestiaries, which show all natural phenomena in relation to the history of human salvation (cf. Thomas Aquinas, below, chapter 5).

17. Readers of Tolkien's other works can compare the dreamer's plight with Smith in Faery, who was right to be there, or with a trespassing mortal on the shores of Eldamar. The aging of a person during what seems like a brief visit in an other world (or even only a glimpse) is a familiar motif in folklore.

18. In the Tolkien chapter of *Modern Heroism* (Berkeley, 1973), passim.

19. Mawer and Stanton's *Place-names of Buckinghamshire* (Cambridge, 1925) says Worminghall must have belonged to a man with the Old English name Wyrma or Wurma. Ekwall's *Oxford Dictionary of English Place-names* says it could be "reptile corner" [they basked

there?]. The village Thame is named for the river it stands on, "Dark [Stream]". Aich Hill is Oak Hill. Tolkien knew all this, of course.

20. A weak king (*roi fainéant*, "do-nothing") is common in French *chansons de geste* about the time following that of Charlemagne. He was invested with all the goodness and energy of kings for several generations, and his descendants pretty much sat on their hands (cf. *La Chanson de Guillaume*, for one).

21. Cf. E. R. Eddison; and Peter Hogarth, *Dragons* (New York, 1979), p. 133.

22. Translated by Gwyn and Thomas Jones (New York, 1949), p. 29.

23. On *Hamlet*, quoted by R. P. Blackmur, "In the Hope of Straightening Things Out," in *T. S. Eliot*, ed. Hugh Kenner (Englewood Cliffs, 1962), p. 144.

24. A like fate befalls Gully Jimson's paintings in Joyce Cary's *The Horse's Mouth* (1944). By Carpenter's biography (pp. 196ff.), it looks as if Tolkien could not have read Cary.

25. Frankenstein is a classic case of this problem. The first thing that monster tried to do was smile. If that artist had stood by his subcreation instead of repudiating it in sudden fright, who knows what good might have been achieved?

26. C. S. Lewis in *Surprised by Joy* speaks at some length of the seductiveness of the occult and the possible horrible consequences of yielding to it (especially p. 163); cf. *The Magician's Nephew* and the Deep Heaven trilogy.

27. Lewis chose the title as a retort to William Blake (1757–1827), who had written *The Marriage of Heaven and Hell*.

28. *Sir Gawain and the Green Knight, Pearl*, and *Sir Orfeo* (Tolkien's translations) (Boston, 1975), p. 18. *The Pearl* would fascinate Tolkien, with its unique combination of feeling and form: a demanding rhyme-scheme kept up for ten sets of ten verses, plus one verse. To work so hard over a poem, the writer must care very much; and indeed, the subject as stated in the poem is gripping: the loss of a little girl not yet two, probably a daughter. Grieving for his lost pearl, the poet dreams of seeing her a grown girl richly robed and decked with pearls; she assures him that she is well and happy—more so even than the dreamer can understand—with Jesus and His friends. The dreamer awakes comforted and resolved to patience for his life on earth. The poem must have been a beacon for Tolkien, with his love of Middle English and elaborate versification, his loneliness and his hope. For more on "Sir Orfeo" and the myth behind it, see chapter 5, note 23.

29. Carpenter, p. 243.

30. In the United States it was published in *Redbook*, December, 1967, as well as by Houghton Mifflin.

31. Edited by Baillie Tolkien (Boston, 1976); unpaginated. The letter quoted is that of 1926; subsequent quotations identify letters by date except the last, which is not dated. The book is referred to as *FCL*.

32. When Tolkien thought of his cycle of mythology for England, he hoped graphic artists would join their work to his ("other minds and hands, wielding paint . . ." [Carpenter, p. 90]). It has happened: artists from the queen of Denmark on down have been drawn to Tolkien's subcreation. Among the published artists have been Tim Kirk, Greg and Tim Hildebrandt, Michael Green, and Joan Wyatt. The artist whose work I find the closest equivalent to Tolkien in her own medium has never illustrated him in her life: Sulamith Wülfing (the Peacock Fantasy Art series has a volume of her work).

33. The cycle was sung by one William Elvin in 1966 at Ronald and Edith Tolkien's golden wedding party. It has been published (Boston, 1967), with material by Tolkien which told more about former ages than *The Lord of the Rings* had. Hereafter cited as *RGEO*.

Chapter Four

1. Carpenter, p. 74.
2. Ibid., p. 86.
3. Ibid., p. 90.
4. Ibid., p. 74.
5. Tolkien speaks strongly against diminutive fairies in "On Fairy Stories" (pp. 5f.); and some of his quotations from Drayton are indeed unprepossessing. However, I am afraid that imagining diminutive races may be an ineradicable human inclination. Acorn cups are so evidently cups—who would use them? Flower petals would be such exquisite textiles, and so on and on.

6. In the "Völundarkvitha" of the *Poetic Edda*, the smith is called an elf. His wife (a swan-valkyrie) leaves him. He is captured, lamed, (cf. Vulcan), and set to work by King Nithuth, whose sons Völund kills, and seduces his daughter, and escapes on wings which he made. Much of this story inspired Tolkien's Eol. The same character appears in the Old English poem *Deor*. A later German sobriquet for the devil was "Junker Voland," which might be the same name. See Carpenter, p. 160.

7. This was still true in the 1960s, when Deborah C. Webster, a visiting American scholar, wrote:

> Now if I had my little VeeWee [Volkswagen] here,
> I should be too un-humble in this street. . . .
> Having a bike, and second-hand at that,
> Now I *belong*; can float off like the others,

Humble and silent as a local cat,
And shameless can salute my two-wheeled brothers. . . .

8. Simonne d'Ardenne, who as a student visited the Tolkien household, remembers the letters as dealing with hobbits ("The Man and the Scholar," in Salu and Farrell, p. 34). Publication of the letters reveals no hobbits in them; Professor d'Ardenne very likely remembers "The Hobbit" being told and discussed in some of the years that letters came from Father Christmas.

9. Parallels between Tolkien's Gondor and Byzantium were shown by Ivor Rogers in a paper at the Conference on Medieval Studies, Kalamazoo, 1971; so Tolkien was conscious of the Eastern Empire.

10. Joe Christopher makes the Green Brother the Christmas spirit of the South Pole; but Tolkien was so much a man of the European hemisphere that the Summer Solstice is more likely ("Christmas at the South Pole," in *The Tolkien Scrapbook*, ed. Alida Becker [New York, 1978], p. 124).

11. Carpenter, p. 172.

12. Ibid., p. 75.

13. Ibid., p. 165.

14. *The Hobbit* (New York, 1965), p. 16. Quotations henceforth identified in the text by *H* and page number.

15. Carpenter, p. 176.

16. Ibid., p. 51.

17. Ibid., p. 176.

18. The name Balin is not on the dwarf list but is that of an Arthurian knight (he of the two swords and the dolorous stroke). Eikinskjaldi (Oakenshield) is listed as the name of a separate dwarf; Tolkien makes it the epithet of Thorin (which means bold). Gandalf is given as a dwarf name, but Tolkien, reflecting that it means "magical elf," gives it to his wizard, originally called Bladorthin. The "Voluspo" ("Sybil's Prophecy") in the *Elder Edda* lists the dwarves, and Snorri recapitulates the list in the first part of his *Prose Edda*. E. L. Epstein suggests that the writers of Disney's *Snow White* might have been looking at ancient dwarf names ("The Novels of J. R. R. Tolkien and the Ethnology of Medieval Christendom," *Philological Quarterly*, October, 1969, p. 518).

19. Carpenter, p. 177.

20. In making himself merely the relayer of a spurious source, Tolkien is following an old tradition. Malory, Wolfram von Eschenbach, and other Arthurian writers have stimulated researchers for hundreds of years by saying their story came from such-and-such a book; in modern times, cf. H. P. Lovecraft's *Necronomicon*.

21. Cf. Bonniejean Christensen, "Gollum's Character Transforma-

tion in *The Hobbit,*" in *A Tolkien Compass,* ed. Lobdell, p. 9–28.

22. London: Thomas Nelson, 1960. The story is also called Hervar's Saga. Tyrfing, the sword in this tale, appears in Poul Anderson's *Broken Sword* (New York, 1971). On Tolkien's riddles, see George Boswell's article in the *Tennessee Folklore Society Bulletin,* 35, no. 2. (1969), 44–49: West's bibliography cross-lists other relevant articles.

23. A ring of invisibility, won by a deed which combines trickery and mercy, is in the fourth canto of Ariosto's *Orlando Furioso.* C. S. Lewis compared Tolkien's work to Ariosto's, and Tolkien retorted, "I don't know Ariosto and I'd loathe him if I did" (Carpenter, p. 218). But about the winning of the ring he might have been amused and pleased. Ariosto is less practical than Tolkien: to be made invisible by the Italian's ring, one had to carry it in one's mouth.

24. It seems odd to readers of *The Lord of the Rings* that Gollum can bear to be parted from the Precious even by leaving it on his island. It tired him to wear and then galled him to carry, we are told (revised *H,* 87); and we see its exhausting effect on Frodo in *The Lord of the Rings.* But in the latter work, even exhaustion is no motive for parting with the Ring. Conceivably it gave Gollum so much leeway because their place was so solitary; also, Sauron was not yet summoning it.

25. Though he does resemble Wagner's Alberich and Mime. Tolkien, steeped in the tales which Wagner too had used for sources, was annoyed when his Ring story was compared with the operas: "Both rings were round, and there the resemblance ceased" (Carpenter, p. 202). An interesting article on Tolkien and Wagner is Robert A. Hall, Jr., "Tolkien's Hobbit Tetralogy as 'Anti-Nibelungen,'" *The Western Humanities Review,* 22 no. 4 (Autumn, 1978), 351–59.

26. Cf. Shippey, "Creation from Philology."

27. Carpenter, p. 178.

28. The late and patchwork (but fascinating) romance *Hrolf Kraki's Saga* has one warrior—Bothvar Bjarki, son of Bjorn and Bera—in a trance while a bear helps his comrades in battle. When a friend wakes him, Bothvar says he never should have done that, and they are defeated. The same saga shows a group of King Hrolf's berserkers; they conform to the modern stereotype of the pea-brained bully. Bothvar befriends the scullion the fighters oppress and makes a hero of him: a refreshing piece of altruism amid the vengeance which forms a practically universal motive in Norse stories. The saga has been translated by Gwyn Jones in *Eirik the Red and Other Icelandic Sagas* (Oxford, 1961) and adapted (faithfully) by Poul Anderson (New York, 1973).

29. Berserk feats have been attributed to the ingestion of psychotropic mushrooms. A worker in a mental hospital before tranquilizers testifies to equivalent feats performed with no stimulant from outside the "berserker's" body.

30. Tolkien's travelers are deprived of their conveyances so regularly, and left to journey on foot, that I believe the situation is a symbol for Tolkien's feeling that human beings in this world are generally left to make their way on their own will and judgment, lacking the feeling of outside help. C. S. Lewis's characters walk less and ride more. Cf. my paper "Vehicles of Transportation in the Fiction of Lewis and Tolkien," given at the Secondary Universe Conference, Queensborough College, 1970.

31. William Green shows that Tolkien probably got the description of the hunt from "Sir Orfeo" rather than any other source. The publication of Tolkien's modern rendering of that romance supports Green. (*"The Hobbit* and Other Fiction by J. R. R. Tolkien: Their Roots in Medieval Heroic Literature and Language"; see Dissertation Abstracts 30, 1970, 4944A.) White creatures in Celtic tales are likely to be otherworldly, especially the white stag of Arthurian romance, cf. *The Mabinogion.*

32. E. B. White's beautifully drawn Charlotte Aranea Cavatica was still fifteen years in the future. See "Tolkien and Spiders," by Bob Mesibov (*Orcrist,* IV [1971], pp. 3–4).

33. This connection of Tolkien's elves with the stars perhaps relates his work to that of Dunsany (1878–1957), whom Tolkien may be setting straight. In *The King of Elfand's Daughter,* Dunsany shows his elves as people of the stars, but in conflict with the author's conception of the godly order for humankind. Dunsany seems not to like his conception of the godly order: stodgy. Tolkien, loving God, sees the divine order as best for every creature, whether elf, human being, or hobbit. His work achieves a uniquely ordered unity between the stodgy (hobbits) and the poetic, beautiful people of the stars.

For a striking picture of the stars as an especial manifestation of God's order, cf. Meredith's "Lucifer in Starlight": ". . . at the stars / Which are the brain of Heaven, he looked, and sank. / Around the ancient track marched, rank on rank, / The army of unalterable law."

On light, dark and black elves, see Jakob Grimm, *Teutonic Mythology* (New York, 1966).

Though Tolkien drops the word "gnomes" from *The Hobbit, The Silmarillion* reveals how he fits it in: human beings in Middle-earth, meeting Finrod the Noldo, named him Nóm, their word for wisdom (*S,* 141). Tolkien is taking "gnome," a word coined by Paracelsus in the

sixteenth century for the race of earth-people, as cognate with the
Greek "gnome" ("wise saying"), gnosis, etc.; all from an Indo-European "knowledge" root whence we still get our silent k in know.

34. The devastating effects of dragons' shrieks are attested in "Lludd
and Llefelys," in *The Mabinogion.*

35. Some readers find the personal asides in *The Hobbit* ("Now
you know enough to go on with," etc.) irritating. But Nature abhors
a vacuum, and why should not Tolkien abhor pretending to write in
one, since the book *was* originally an oral narrative? Randel Helms
is rare in realizing that in style as well as content, "what Tolkien
has done . . . is altogether suitable for children, and there is no use
faulting him" (*Tolkien's World* [Boston, 1974], p. 27).

36. Critical opinions differ again on Tolkien's verse. One good
article on it is Mary Quella Kelly's "The Poetry of Fantasy," which
bears in mind the relation of the poems to their setting (in Isaacs and
Zimbardo, *Tolkien and the Critics* [Notre Dame, 1968], pp. 170–200)

37. Tolkien's names have been widely commented upon. The lead-
ing article is his own, "Nomenclature in *The Lord of the Rings*" (in
A Tolkien Compass, ed. Jared Lobdell [La Salle, 1975], pp. 155–201).
An example of a superior fantasist with not-so-good names is Patricia
McKillip.

38. Grotta-Kurska, p. 104.

Chapter Five

1. Alfred, Lord Tennyson and Pierre Teilhard de Chardin are
but two modern instances of people in whose minds Genesis and
geology have generated remarkable results.

2. Figures given on III, 479. For Holmes and astronomy, see "A
Study in Scarlet," chap. 2.

3. E. g., the Howes and Orr articles mentioned in note 6 to the
preface; also Marcella Juhren, "The Ecology of Middle-earth" (*Mythlore,* 2, no. 1 [1970; equals *Tolkien Journal,* 12], 4–6). A rare dissenting voice is a meteorologist's: Samuel S. Long, letter in *Mythlore,* 9
(1973), 21.

4. Carpenter, p. 274. The translation he heard used in daily life
would have been the Douay or one of its revisions. Imagination suggests why perhaps Tolkien was involved with the Jerusalem Bible. In
1961—before so much interdenominational mistrust was flushed away—
the Anglican Church had issued the New English Bible, now one of
the respected translations. Among its contributors was John Masefield:
not only the poet laureate of England at the time, but the author of

an outstanding juvenile fantasy, *The Midnight Folk.* Its sequel, *The Box of Delights,* is far inferior, and much too similar to T. H. White's *Sword in the Stone.* Seeing Masefield's name on the New English Bible, Roman Catholics can be imagined gulping, "Whom can WE get to balance HIM?" and answering, "Tolkien!"

5. *Summa Theologica,* pt. 1, question 1, art. 10.

6. Lin Carter connects Earendil with the Norse Orwendil (J. B. Cabell's Horvendile), a giant whose frozen toe was turned into a star. *Kalki,* 3, no. 3 (Summer, 1969), 85–87; also see previous article, same issue.

7. C. S. Lewis, writing in a period when scientific determinism was considered modern and valid, gleefully pointed out that in the sixteenth century too there was a scientific-determinist school of thought: believers in astrology. (Introduction to *English Literature in the Sixteenth Century* [Oxford, 1954].)

8. Job 38:7, Douai translation. Blake's illustrations of *Job* include a beauty for this verse.

9. Carpenter, p. 170.

10. Idem.

11. *The Dialogues of Plato,* trans. B. Jowett (Oxford, 1953, fourth ed.), III, 713.

12. One sampling out of many Atlantis tales is Lin Carter's anthology *The Magic of Atlantis* (New York, 1970).

13. It is so in the Septuagint Greek and the Vulgate Latin, the bases of many later translations. A modern Rabbi takes them to be outsized human beings, very likely reported by short human beings. Asked about the suggestion of miscarriage, he speculated that a very large baby might not be carried to term. (Or those reporting might have thought them so ugly as to call them "abortions.")

14. Grimm, *Teutonic Mythology,* p. 372.

15. Carpenter, p. 184. Readers who feel eye-split by Fëanor's seven sons Maedhros, Maglor, Celegorm, Caranthir, Curufin, Amrod, and Amras should reflect on Queen Maeve in the *Tain Bo Cuailgne,* whose seven sons are all named Maine, each with a descriptive surname.

16. C. S. Lewis gives a fine example of the twentieth-century method which Tolkien does not use: "Jane thought she was annoyed because her hair was not going up to her liking and because Mark was fussing. She also knew, of course [of course!] that she was deeply angry with herself. . . . But she thought this anger was only in the back of her mind, and had no suspicion that it was pulsing through every vein and producing at that very moment the clumsiness in her fingers which

made her hair seem intractable" (*That Hideous Strength* [New York, 1965], p. 46).

17. *The Silmarillion* (Boston, 1977), p. 170. Hereafter cited as *S*.

18. E.g., *Tobit*; Luke 1–2. These creatures are called angels, from the Greek word for messenger. Undefined words in the Bible (e.g., "principalities and powers") have allowed scholars and speculators to envisage nine choirs of angels: Seraphim, Cherubim, Thrones; Dominions, Virtues, Powers; Principalities, Archangels, Angels. Fallen angels would then also be of nine kinds, unless a whole tenth choir fell, as shown in some medieval paintings with nine circles and a blank. (Since ten was considered a perfect number, they thought God would have started with ten.) See *The Celestial Hierarchies* of Dionysius the Areopagite (Pseudo-Dionysius; Fintry, 1965) and *A Dictionary of Angels*, ed. Gustave Davidson (New York, 1967). Mainstream Judaism and Christianity downplay angels (as they do other worlds, see chapter 3), for several reasons. It would be easy for human beings to worship them disproportionately; Lewis speaks of the planetary angel of Jupiter, "through whom the joy of creation principally blows across these fields . . . in old times . . . by fatal but not inexplicable misprision, confused with his Maker" (*That Hideous Strength*, p. 327). Overstress on angels could tempt a student to two great heresies: gnosticism, the idea that some rarefied knowledge is needed for salvation; and dualism, a belief in two gods, which often calls matter bad.

19. Aelfric says that before mankind sinned, the sun was seven times brighter and the moon was bright as the sun is now (Anglo-Saxon homily, "De Falsis Diis").

20. Cf. Saint Augustine, "Thou hast made us for Thyself, oh Lord, and our hearts are restless until they rest in Thee" (*Confessions*, bk. 1, chap. 1). Also cf. George Herbert, "The Pulley."

> When God at first made man,
> Having a glass of blessings standing by;
> Let us (said he) pour on him all we can. . . .
>
> When almost all was out, God made a stay,
> Perceiving that alone of all his treasure
> Rest at the bottom lay.
>
> For if I should (said he)
> Bestow this jewell also on my creature,
>
> He would adore my gifts instead of me,

And rest in Nature, not the God of Nature:
So both should losers be.

Yet let him keep the rest,
But keep them with repining restlessness:
Let him be rich and weary, that at least,
If goodness lead him not, yet weariness
May toss him to my breast.

21. Lewis in *Out of the Silent Planet* imagines a wholesome attitude of a mortal race toward death, shown in the hross's conversation
with Ransom and at the hross funeral (pp. 75, 131f., 159).

22. Everything can be perceived as through a scrim of either beauty
or disgust. A striking double portrait of a city from each point of
view can be found near the end of Saunders Anne Laubenthal's
Excalibur (New York, 1973).

23. The Volsungs, the lines of Laius and Tantalus, and the Finnish
Kullervo are obvious analogues. In medieval England, the romance
of Sir Dégaré is an anti-Oedipus in a Christian setting: the hero
comes within a hair of sleeping with his mother and killing his father,
but each time the characters get their identities straight in time,
because God "wold not that they synnyd" (Rumble, *Breton Lays*,
p. 64).

24. Do not look in medieval fiction for grisly werewolf stories.
Marie de France's "Bisclavret" and the romance of William of Palermo
(Guillaume de Palerne) both have *good* werewolves.

25. It is one theme rather well picked up by the movie of *The
Lord of the Rings*.

26. The Greek myth of Orpheus and Eurydice, a separation by
death and a search for death's defeat, ends tragically: Opheus's music
can win her from the Lord of the Dead, but Orpheus lacks the will
power to keep his eyes off her. But the medieval romance "Sir Orfeo,"
which Tolkien translated, written since Christ's redemption of the
world, has Orfeo successfully rescue Heurodis (cf. Dégaré, above,
note 23, for another A.D. adaptation of a B.C. story).

Tolkien, who needed no myth to inform him that a dear and important lady was dead, seems to have been attracted to the Orpheus
story. He too was moved by music, though he did not follow his
mother in playing the piano, but made his music with words. (Cf.
Anthony Ugolnik, "*Wordhord Onleac*: the Medieval Sources of J. R. R.
Tolkien's Linguistic Aesthetic," *Mosaic*, 10, no. 2 [1977], 13–32. Elvish sings itself and the Black Speech chokes itself.) A semilegendary
Tolkien ancestor had been a harpsichordist; and Edith's piano playing

would have been part of her attractiveness. In *The Silmarillion*, Tolkien shows music as both the vehicle of creation and the weapon which overcomes the Dread Lord.

27. One theory may be found in the "Orcs' Marching Song" in *A Tolkien Scrapbook*, ed. Alida Becker (New York, 1978), p. 146. Poul Anderson in *The Broken Sword* goes into some detail about the breeding of a changeling; his elves are not like Tolkien's.

28. David Miller, "The Moral Universe of J. R. R. Tolkien," in *Mankato Studies* (1967), p. 62.

29. Cf. Paracelsus, *Liber de Nymphis* . . . Legend has it that elementals are soulless, but can gain a soul by marrying a human being. Fouqué's nineteenth-century fairy-tale *Undine* and Giraudoux' twentieth-century play *Ondine* deal with a human-nymph marriage; they are loosely based on the medieval romance *Der Ritter von Stauffenberg*. Goldberry resembles Milton's goddess of the River Severn:

> Sabrina fair,
> Listen where thou art sitting
> Under the glassy, cool, translucent wave,
> In twisted braids of lilies knitting
> The loose train of thy amber-dropping hair. . . .
>
> Comus

However, Sabrina was not born a nymph, but a human being.

30. Letter to Dr. Herbert Schiro, *Mythlore*, 10 (2, no. 2, 1975), 19.

31. In *Time and Tide*, December 3, 1955, p. 1561. And see Brendan in *Lives of the Saints*, trans J. F. Webb (Harmondsworth, 1965).

32. *That Hideous Strength*, p. 283.

33. Carpenter, pp. 89–90.

Chapter Six

1. L. Frank Baum's *Wizard of Oz* and Edgar Rice Burroughs's *Tarzan* and science-fiction books spawned scores of successors; set in the primary world, Arthur Ransome's *Swallows and Amazons* was followed by related adventures. Squads of writers under a "house name" could continue a juvenile series out of sight: the Bobsey Twins, Tom Swift, Cherry Ames, and all. The growing-up of one well-liked character could furnish four books easily and more when squeezed: Rebecca of Sunnybrook Farm, Anne of Green Gables. A too well-liked character could force an author's hand, as Sherlock Holmes and Ayesha did to Conan Doyle and Rider Haggard: each had to be resurrected by popular demand.

2. Carpenter, p. 185.

3. Ibid., p. 188.

4. Ibid., p. 186.

5. Sauron is thus comparable to many an ogre of folklore whose soul is in a separate object. He has been called an abstraction of evil, but his superficial reading cannot stand since Paul Kocher included a character-study of Sauron in *Master of Middle-earth* (Boston, 1972).

6. W. H. Auden has written several articles about Tolkien's use of the Quest motif; cf. the mythological researches of Joseph Campbell, and Anne C. Petty's study of Tolkien's mythology, *One Ring to Bind Them All* (University Ala., 1979).

7. Richard C. West, "Progress Report on the Variorum Tolkien," *Orcrist* 4, pp. 6–7; this article is the source for the six book titles and the quotation.

8. Outstanding examples are Ursula K. LeGuin's *A Wizard of Earthsea, The Tombs of Atuan,* and *The Farthest Shore*; and Patricia McKillip's *The Riddlemaster of Hed, Heir of Sea And Fire,* and *Harpist in the Wind*; also works by Vera Chapman, C. J. Cherryh, Piers Anthony, Steven Donaldson, and others.

The title of Tolkien's whole book, *The Lord of the Rings,* has raised queries, because why name it after its prime antagonist when the heroes are more interesting and more focal? (Why call a book Hitler when it is about Tommy Atkins and Churchill?) This does not mean the book is about World War II; it is not. As to interesting characters, Colin Manlove finds Sauron disproportionately fascinating, so he would probably agree with the title (*Modern Fantasy,* rev. ed. [Cambridge, 1978]). It has been suggested that the title refers to God, Lord of the planets in their orbits. I reflected that a Lord was the opposite of an addict, so a Ring-lord would be any character who could part with or refuse the Ring. However, Tolkien's text leaves no doubt that Sauron *is* meant: Tolkien's title is shortened from Frodo's "The Downfall of the Lord of the Rings and the Return of the King" (III, 380; cf. Elrond's statement that the title belongs to Sauron only [I, 298]).

9. Cf. Douglas Grey, "Chaucer and 'Pite,' " in Salu and Farrell, *J. R. R. Tolkien, Scholar and Storyteller,* pp. 173–203.

10. A finely balanced consideration of the subject is Nan C. Scott, "War and Pacifism in *The Lord of the Rings,*" *Tolkien Journal,* 15, (Summer 1972), 23–30.

11. Tolkien himself did not know at that point who the character was. Trotter the hobbit became Strider the ranger and at last Aragorn the king. Kocher's study of his character is particularly good.

12. E.g., Jan Wojcik in "Samwise—Halfwise? or, Who Is the Hero of *The Lord of the Rings?*" *Tolkien Journal,* 3, no. 2 (1967), 16–18.

13. Carpenter, p. 81.

14. Clyde S. Kilby, *Tolkien and the Silmarillion* (Wheaton, Ill., 1976), p. 31.

15. Preface to *George Macdonald, an Anthology*. Reprinted as introduction to *Phantastes* and *Lilith* (London, 1962).

16. Compare C. S. Lewis's remark about the Inklings, that the group is provided with all the estates, "except of course anyone who could actually produce a single necessity of life—a loaf, a boot, or a hut" (Kilby, p. 69).

17. Carpenter, p. 186.

18. Ibid., p. 160.

19. As observed by Louise Morrison, *J. R. R. Tolkien's Fellowship of the Ring* (New York, 1976), p. 34.

20. Proverbs 8:22–31. This was a regular liturgical reading for the feast of the Annunciation, March 25 (see below; Ronald and Edith Tolkien's wedding day was March 22). For play as every creature's proper activity, cf. Kipling's creation myth in "The Crab that Played with the Sea" (*Just So Stories*); Johan Huizinga, *Homo Ludens*; Harvey Cox, *The Feast of Fools*. One could suggest that only Morgoth introduced the idea that there was anything to do but play. If Tom is indeed that Wisdom and if the Dark Lord he refers to is Morgoth, that answers the vexed question of whether he is older than the ents, who are also called eldest: Tom has been on earth longer. The ents are the oldest race, Tom the oldest person.

21. Barliman (Butterbur), host at Bree, sounds like Barlennan, captain of the *Bree*, in Hal Clement's *Mission of Gravity*. Tolkien's work was published later; it is unlikely that either author read the other's mind while composing: a warning to eager half-baked source-hunters.

22. He all but uses C. S. Lewis's touchstone line for a bad magician, "Ours is a high and lonely destiny"; and again in bk. 3, chap. 10. (Cf. *The Magician's Nephew* and the Deep Heaven trilogy.)

23. Aragorn was not at the feast because he was at a council of war with Arwen's brothers Elladan and Elrohir. For another El dynasty which harries orcs, cf. Spenser: "[Elfiline's] son was *Elfinell* who overcame / The wicked *Gobbelines* in bloudy field" (*Faerie Queene*, II, x, 73). Elros and Elrond, twin sons of the star, perhaps correspond to Castor and Pollux, twin sons now stars. (So do C. S. Lewis's princes Cor and Corin, the horseman and the boxer, in *The Horse and His Boy*.)

24. Cf. my "Everyclod and Everyhero," in *A Tolkien Compass*, ed. Jared Lobdell (LaSalle, Ill., 1978).

25. The absence of large animals in Tolkien's world has been noted as strange for the epoch described. Wolves are the biggest wild thing, unless one counts the wild kine of Araw, far away eastward, or the oliphaunts to the south. Had Tolkien lived longer in South Africa, he would probably have written in more major fauna. (Cf. Anthony Dent, *Lost Beasts of Britain* [London, 1974].)

26. Cf. note to preface on worship. Gimli has what Charles Williams calls a Beatrician experience (after Dante and Beatrice): seeing the wonder of God suddenly revealed in a creature; which is how the Creator wanted creatures to see each other. Cf. *The Figure of Beatrice* (London, 1943); and *Taliessin through Logres, The Region of the Summer Stars,* and C. S. Lewis's *Arthurian Torso,* 1 vol. ed. (Grand Rapids, 1974).

27. Lewis is similarly scrupulous in giving his characters choices. Tolkien has been called either bloodthirsty or a political extremist for sanctioning the killing of orcs, though they are speaking beings. *The Silmarillion* shows why: Morgoth so brainwashed, genewashed, and God-knows-what his captive elves, bound them with such a determinism, that orcs do not have the freedom of choice proper to any creature correctly called person. Kocher's *Master of Middle-earth* is particularly sound on will.

28. Karen Rockow "Funeral Customs in Tolkien," (*Unicorn*, 2, no. 3 [Winter, 1973], 22–30). Tolkien's three-part dirge to the winds recalls that in *The Song of Igor's Campaign.*

29. Richard C. West, "The Interlace and Professor Tolkien: Medieval Narrative Technique in *The Lord of the Rings,*" *Orcrist*, I, pp. 26–49). Revised and reprinted in Lobdell's *Tolkien Compass.*

30. Cf. my article on the use of color in the fiction of Tolkien and Lewis, forthcoming in *Orcrist* (probably no. 9). Though black is the color of Mordor, it is also the royal color of Gondor. Frodo sees Arwen's dark beauty as fashioned on purpose: "Now . . . night too shall be beautiful and beloved and all its fear pass away" (III, 310). Edith Tolkien had dark hair.

A touching note on personal coloring is that though Tolkien's eyes were blue—celebrated endlessly in our literature—he makes very little fuss over blue eyes. Only Bombadil's blue eye peeking unconquerably through the Ring is emphasized to counter Sauron's red one. But Edith's eyes were grey, and a great proportion of her husband's best characters have grey eyes. Hobbits' eyes are often brown.

31. Carpenter, p. 194; conversely, Lewis's Ransom is partly based on Tolkien (Carpenter, p. 170).

32. An ent was seen in the Shire, but the observer was not believed (I, 73). Besides knowing the Anglo-Saxon Genesis account of "entas" on Earth in those days, Tolkien of course also knew the Gospel story of the man with his sight partway restored, who said, "I see men like trees walking" (Mark 8:24).

33. His special water adds three inches to their growth. Cf. Lewis's refreshments for tree-people in *Prince Caspian*.

34. Many a parent in the primary world can sympathize with the ent wives' desire for "peace," defined as things staying where they are put.

35. Carpenter, pp. 27–28.

36. There is also the biographical-sociological explanation in reply to "no women": Taine's *race, milieu, et moment*. Certainly much of the action in Tolkien's stories of war and fellowship is among males; much of Tolkien's *experience* of war and fellowship was among males (cf. *Watership Down* again). He had no sister, lost his mother at twelve, and was forbidden to see Edith. Romance was something in a book unless it was his own, and that was *private*. Cameraderie between men and women was not very common in his culture (exception: Professor and Mrs. Wright [Carpenter, pp. 56, 155]). Jonathan Gathorne-Hardy, writing about the men of English "public" boarding schools at that time, goes as far as to say approximately "in eveything but their sex lives, they were homosexual" (*The Old Scool Tie*); of course, Tolkien was not at a boarding school. Anyway, both sexes are very nice and very various, and there is nothing weird about liking a sex even if one is a member of it.

37. "Men, Halflings and Hero Worship," *Niekas*, June, 1966, pp. 25–44. The article is reprinted, but cut, in Isaacs and Zimbardo, *Tolkien and the Critics* (Notre Dame, 1968).

38. Psychological critics will be delighted to find an ego, an id and a superego walking along in a row.

39. Cf. Marion Parret, "Rings off Their Fingers; Hands in The Lord of the Rings." *Ariel*, 6, 4 (1975), pp. 52–66.

40. Faber Birren states that a person who loves grey has probably worked hard at reforming their character. Unfortunately, Birren cites no documentation (*Color* [New Hyde Park, N.Y., 1963]).

41. Spiders do not have faceted eyes such as Tolkien attributes to Shelob (see for instance Mesibov, "Tolkien and Spiders"). Tolkien's putative aversion to spiders may indeed have prevented his observing closely; but, also, the scene described puts him under some constraint, whether or not he knew arachnid anatomy: eight

little beady black eyes would simply not deal with the star-glass's radiance so wonderfully as do two bulgy prismatic eyes.

42. Unlike Spenser, the composer of the *Tain bo Cuilnge*, Vergil, Homer, and others. Ancient epics were repositories of history, as well as tales; and writers of newer epics thought it right to imitate them in their catalogues and historical excursions. Whether *The Lord of the Rings* is an epic is a debate I am not entering, but they do have features in common.

43. An old weapon which evaporates in its opponent's blood was Beowulf's giant-sword after he had used it on Grendel's mother. Aragorn can tell that Frodo's dagger only cut the wraith's cloak on Weathertop, for "all blades perish that pierce that dreadful king" (I, 265). The morgul-knife vanishes in the daylight.

44. Any healer will get crowded upon; the doctor at a party is a byword. Granted, both Aragorn and Christ are "the one who is to come" in their story; but they are not the same kind of savior. Christ clearly said His kingdom was not of this world, whereas Aragorn's is (cf. "Everyclod and Everyhero").

45. Of course the gardener's ideal is a rose, as Richard Mathews noticed (*Lightning from a Clear Sky* [Van Nuys, Calif., 1978], p. 41). It is Western culture's symbolic flower par excellence (the East has its lotus). In the thirteenth-century *Roman de la Rose*, Guillaume de Loris uses it to stand for love and Jean de Meun for sex. Dante on his trip to Heaven found in the center the Rose of the Communion of Saints.

46. Beckett's *Waiting for Godot* (of all dissimilar works) shows comparable pairs: Pozzo and Lucky, oppressor and slave, are in worse condition in act 2 (blind and dumb); Vladimir and Estragon, friends, are slightly better off (shoes fit).

47. So that even before *The Silmarillion* was published, persistent students had doped out a good deal of the history, e.g., Foster, Kocher, and Tyler.

48. A genre of fiction which sometimes allows itself outstanding exploration of setting is science fiction, which Jack Lewis enjoyed reading and discussing, and wrote himself. Hal Clement and Frank Herbert, for two, build their secondary worlds with beautiful thoroughness. The explorations of science fiction, however, are usually confined to one period in the history of their setting. Tolkien has plunged deep into the history of his world, as well as leading us step by step across its leagues; and he is uniquely acquainted with its languages and therefore its peoples. Since the publication of his fiction, science fiction has expanded its explorations; thorough-

ness is possible, fast surface action not the only necessity. Marion Zimmer Bradley, cited as a Tolkienist, keeps increasing her history of Darkover.

Tolkien and Lewis once agreed to write stories of space-travel (*CSL*) and time-travel (*JRRT*) leading to the discovery of Myth (Carpenter, p. 170). Lewis duly came out with his Deep Heaven trilogy (or Ransom trilogy): *Out of the Silent Planet* (1938), *Perelandra* (1944), *That Hideous Strength* (1946). His never-finished *Dark Tower* (ed. Walter Hooper [New York, 1977]) looks like his attempt at a time-travel book, begun when Tolkien was not coming out with his. Tolkien never finished the books he started in response to the project, but his whole work is his answer.

Chapter Seven

1. Not abstract, which properly means abstracted from something in the primary world, like one of Picasso's flying lines abstracted—via a distorted drawing and a careful drawing—from a runner.

2. Fantasy artists' relaxed certainty about the reality of the world goes with a comparable certainty about their own aesthetic inclinations. Fantasy art is well known for portraying things which are easy to like (castles, trees, etc.), by contrast with Ashcan realism. (Cf. Robert Pirsig, *Zen and the Art of Motorcycle Maintenance*: "Quality is 'just' what you like.") There is a similar certainty in the moral sphere; "A man's good judgment for Tolkien, as for the [American] founding fathers, is based on self-evident truths" (Mathews, *Lightning*, p. 34). Cf. the biblical description of the just man: "The law of his God is written in his heart."

3. More documents of the time: Albert, Camus, *L'Etranger* (1942); Jean-Paul Sartre, *La Nausee* (1938); and Eliot's *Waste Land* (1922). Of course Tolkien was not the only writer who hoped. The German poet Rilke, who felt the autumn leaves, his planet, and his own body "falling away from every other world into loneliness"—a nauseous perception, surely—recalled that "yet there is One who holds all this falling with endless tenderness in His hands."

> Die Blätter fallen, fallen wie von weit. . . .
> Sie fallen mit verneinender Gebärde.
> Und in den Nächten fällt die schwere Erde
> Aus allen Sternen in die Einsamkeit.
> Wir alle fallen. Diese Hand da fällt.
> Und sieh' dir andere an: es ist in allen.
> Und doch ist Einer, welcher dieses Fallen
> Unendlich sanft in seinen Händen hält.

The leaves are falling, falling as if from far away. . . . They fall with a gesture of denial. And in the nights this heavy Earth is falling out from all the stars into loneliness. We all are falling. This very hand is falling. And look at others: it is in all. And yet there is One who holds all this falling with endless tenderness in His hands. (My translation)

4. Sartre is not just a victim of Roquentin's nausea, any more than Chateaubriand was just a victim of the same syndrome as his romantic character René, who embodied the unease of *his* time. Roquentin's final page sounds oddly as if he longed to write *The Lord of the Rings*: not a history, but "Une autre espèce de livre. Je ne sais pas très bien laquelle—mais il faudrait qu'on devine . . . derrière les pages, quelque chose qui n'existerait pas, qui serait au-dessus de l'existence. Une histoire, par exemple, comme il ne peut pas en arriver, une aventure. II faudrait qu'elle soit belle et dure comme de l'acier et qu'elle fasse honte aux gens de leur existence" ("Another kind of book. I'm not sure what kind, but the reader should sense, beyond its pages, something which would not exist: something above existence. A story, maybe—an impossible one, an adventure. It would have to be as beautiful and hard as steel and make people ashamed of their existence" [Paris, 1938], p. 222).

5. God's covenant with Noah (Genesis 8:22) was partly to reassure the human race that the rule of the seasons is not our responsibility.

6. Raymond A. Schroth, S.J., in *America*, February 18, 1967, p. 254.

7. Kocher, *Master of Middle-earth*, p. 55, italics mine.

8. Cf. Carpenter, p. 31.

9. A religion which emphasizes only the existence and transcendence of the Deity can leave its adherents in the position of the "faith-healer of Deal,/ Who said, 'Although pain isn't real,/ When I sit on a pin/ And it punctures my skin,/ I dislike what I fancy I feel.'"

Orthodox Christianity testifies, on the contrary, that in Jesus the Transcendent itself, in historical time, had a skin, had it punctured, disliked the feeling bitterly, and subsequently was very well, scarred skin and all.

10. Tolkien's manner of enjoying the beauties of nature was pausing to look at them. Once Lewis knew this was Tolkien's way, he stopped inviting him on walking trips, accusing Tolkien of "strolling" rather than properly "walking" (Carpenter, *Inklings*).

11. Norse proverb, "Bare is brotherless back." Tolkien of course had a literal brother in Hilary.

12. Cf. Rogers, "Everyclod and Everyhero." Tolkien's view of deepening gloom, contradicted by an unlikely figure, can be compared to that of the French playwright Jean Giraudoux, who descended from effervescent though ironic hope to deep though effervescent sadness: *Amphitryon 38* (1929); *La Guerre de Troie n'aura pas lieu* (1935); *Ondine* (1939); *Sodome et Gomorrhe,* (1943). Giraudoux too uses all the mythology he knows to write about the world. He came to feel that neither men and women, nor man and nature, nor France and Germany could ever be lovingly espoused. Yet after waning hope, his posthumous *Folle de Chaillot* (1945) shows the victory of the small and mad over the great and greedy. Imagine his Countess Aurelia entertaining Frodo at tea in her cellar.

Selected Bibliography

PRIMARY SOURCES

The Adventures of Tom Bombadil. London: Allen and Unwin, 1962; Boston: Houghton Mifflin, 1962. Reprinted in *The Tolkien Reader*. New York: Ballantine, 1966.

"*Beowulf*: the Monsters and the Critics." [Lecture, 1936.] Reprinted in *An Anthology of Beowulf Criticism*. Edited by Lewis E. Nicholson. Notre Dame: University of Notre Dame Press, 1963. Also in *The Beowulf Poet*. Edited by Donald K. Fry. Twentieth Century Views Series. Englewood Cliffs: Prentice-Hall, 1968.

"On Fairy Stories." [Lecture, 1939]. Reprinted in *Essays Presented to Charles Williams*. Edited by C. S. Lewis. London: Oxford University Press, 1947. Paperback, Grand Rapids: Eerdmans, 1966. Also in *Tree and Leaf*. London: Allen and Unwin, 1964; *The Tolkien Reader*. New York: Ballantine, 1966.

Farmer Giles of Ham. London: Allen and Unwin, 1949. Reprinted in *The Tolkien Reader*. New York: Ballantine, 1966. Reprinted with *Smith of Wootton Major*. New York: Ballantine, 1969.

The Father Christmas Lettters. Edited by Baillie Tolkien. London: Allen and Unwin, 1976; Boston: Houghton Mifflin, 1976.

The Hobbit. London: Allen and Unwin, 1937; rev. ed., 1951; 2d rev. ed., 1966. Boston: Houghton Mifflin, 1938. Paperback, New York: Ballantine, 1965.

"The Homecoming of Beohtnoth Beorhthelm's Son." *Essays and Studies of the English Association*, New Series 6 (1953), 1–18. [Magazine publication, 1953]. Reprinted in *The Tolkien Reader*. New York: Ballantine, 1966.

"Leaf by Niggle." *The Dublin Review*, 432 (Jan. 1945), 46–61. [Magazine publication, 1945]. Reprinted in *Tree and Leaf*. London: Allen and Unwin, 1964. Included in *The Tolkien Reader*. New York: Ballantine, 1966.

The Lord of the Rings. 3 vols. Vol. 1: *The Fellowship of the Ring*. London: Allen and Unwin, 1954; Boston: Houghton Mifflin, 1954. Unauthorized paperback, New York: Ace, 1965. Authorized paperback with revisions, New York: Ballantine, 1965. Vol. 2: *The Two Towers*. London: Allen and Unwin, 1954;

Boston: Houghton Mifflin, 1955. Paperbacks as above. Vol. 3:
The Return of the King. London: Allen and Unwin, 1955; Boston: Houghton Mifflin, 1955. Paperbacks as above.

The Road Goes Ever On. Words by Tolkien and music by Donald Swann. London: Allen and Unwin, 1967; Boston: Houghton Mifflin, 1967.

The Silmarillion. Edited Christopher Tolkien. London: Allen and Unwin, 1977; Boston: Houghton Mifflin, 1977. Paperback, New York: Ballantine, 1979.

Sir Gawain and the Green Knight. Edited by J. R. R. Tolkien and E. V. Gordon. Oxford: Clarendon Press, 1925. Revised edition by Norman Davis (1967).

Sir Gawain and the Green Knight, Pearl, and Sir Orfeo. Translated, with some commentary, by J. R. R. Tolkien and prepared for publication by Christopher Tolkien. London: Allen and Unwin, 1975; Boston: Houghton Mifflin, 1975.

Smith of Wootton Major. London: Allen and Unwin, 1967; Boston: Houghton Mifflin, 1967. Reprinted in paperback with *Farmer Giles of Ham.* New York: Ballantine, 1969.

SECONDARY SOURCES

1. Books and Articles

BECKER, ALIDA, ed. *The Tolkien Scrapbook.* Philadelphia: Running Press, 1978. Mixed bag of solid material, fannish material, and artwork. Noteworthy among the contents are: W. H. AUDEN, "At the End of the Quest, Victory" (review of *The Return of the King*); and JOAN McCLUSKY, "J. R. R. Tolkien: a Short Biography" (perpetuates many of Grotta-Kurska's errors and adds some new ones along with its valid material.)

BRADLEY, MARION ZIMMER. *Men, Halflings and Hero Worship.* Baltimore, T-K Graphics, 1973. This is the whole essay; the version in Isaacs (below) is badly cut. Bradley shows *The Lord of the Rings* chronicling "the end of the Heroic Age in the individual, as well as in Middle-earth."

CARPENTER, HUMPHREY. *Tolkien.* Boston: Houghton Mifflin, 1977. The authorized biography, written with access to Tolkien's papers. Full, charitable, and absorbing.

————. *The Inklings.* Boston: Houghton Mifflin, 1979. Same virtues. A little more about Tolkien, and much about C. S. Lewis and Charles Williams, plus other friends and surroundings.

CARTER, LIN. *Tolkien: a Look Behind The Lord of the Rings.* New York: Ballantine, 1969. Carter's gifts to the field of Fantasy as lover and editor are peerless; as a scholar, he is half-baked. This book contains many excellent leads and considerable distortion.

CASTELL, DAPHNE. "The Realms of Tolkien." *New Worlds,* November, 1966. Reprinted in *Carandaith,* vol. 1, no. 2 (1969) pp. 10–15, 27. Interview with a former student. Tolkien partly fills in the story of Queen Berúthiel.

DAY, DAVID et al. *A Tolkien Bestiary.* New York: Ballantine, 1979. Alphabetical and indexed entries for flora and fauna; tables of chronology and race-distribution. Pictures of things, beings and events, some in color. More for the coffee table than the library carrel. Fun.

DeCAMP, L. SPRAGUE. "White Wizard in Tweeds." *Fantastic,* November 1976, pp. 69–89, 122. Deals with Tolkien, his setting, his books, and their reception.

Diplomat Magazine, 18, no. 197 (October, 1966). Recipes, some art-work, and "Tolkien on Tolkien" (p. 39), about the genesis of his works, namely, his love of language. Also, Aubrey Menen, "Learning to Love the Hobbits" (pp. 32ff.): the books, though "twerpish," involve and impress the reader with their sense of reality.

ELLWOOD, GRACIA FAY. *Good News from Tolkien's Middle Earth.* Grand Rapids: Eerdmans, 1970. Two essays, "Everything Is Alive" and "The Good Guys." The first mentions some psychic phenomena under study currently as possibly being related to phenomena in Tolkien's stories; the second especially studies Bombadil, Gandalf, Frodo, and Aragorn.

EVANS, ROBLEY. *J. R. R. Tolkien.* Writers for the 70's series. New York: Warner Paperback Library, 1972. I find his style hard to wade through. Tolkien's great interest is power, and his great power is his imagination. Discusses the Quest, outer and inner, personal and social. *The Lord of the Rings* is "joyful" and hope-renewing.

FOSTER, ROBERT. *The Complete Guide to Middle-earth.* New York: Ballantine, 1978; paperback 1979. Supersedes Foster's *Guide to Middle-earth* (paperbacks, Mirage, 1971; Ballantine, 1974). Alphabetical listing of names of persons, places, and things from *The Hobbit* through *The Silmarillion.* Also contains chronologies, genealogies, and a table for converting pages between paperback and hardback editions. Full, accurate, and useful.

FULLER, EDMUND et al. *Myth, Allegory and Gospel.* Minneapolis:

Bethany Fellowship, 1974. Lectures on various Fantasy writers
in a Christian perspective, including Kilby on Tolkien.
GROTTA-KURSKA, DANIEL. *J. R. R. Tolkien: Architect of Middle
Earth*. Philadelphia: Running Press, 1976. A journalist working
in adverse circumstances to provide a biography which was
lacking. Pleasant anecdotal material. Riddled with inaccuracies
of spelling, emphasis, and fact. Grotta-Kurska on religion in
The Lord of the Rings (pp. 90–91) is almost as funny as Grotta-
Kurska's typesetter rendering Shelob as Shoebob (p. 102).
HELMS, RANDEL. *Tolkien's World*. Boston: Houghton Mifflin, 1974.
Uneven but interesting. Freudianism is not a very helpful angle
for Tolkien criticism. Fine on the humor of *The Adventures of
Tom Bombadil*.
HILLEGAS, MARK, ed. *Shadows of Imagination*. rev. ed. Carbondale:
Southern Illinois University Press, 1979. Essays on C. S. Lewis
and Charles Williams; includes Charles Moorman, "Now En-
tertain Conjecture of a Time"—the Fictive Worlds of C. S.
Lewis and J. R. R. Tolkien" (Lewis's didacticism can overshadow
his art; not Tolkien's).
ISAACS, NEIL D., and ZIMBARDO, ROSE A., eds. *Tolkien and the Critics*.
Notre Dame: University of Notre Dame Press, 1968. Outstand-
ing collection of essays; contains, among others, articles by W. H.
Auden, Marion Zimmer Bradley, C. S. Lewis, Charles Moorman,
Roger Sale, and Edmund Wilson.
KILBY, CLYDE S. *Tolkien and the Silmarillion*. Wheaton, Ill.: Harold
Shaw, 1976. Short, personal and interesting. Kilby spent a
summer trying to aid the delivery of *The Silmarillion*. (Also see
his article in Hillegas, above.)
KOCHER, PAUL H. *Master of Middle-earth*. Boston: Houghton Mifflin,
1972. One of the two best single-author books on Tolkien's fiction.
Delicate, lucid, and penetrating. Especially good on will, and
on character (Strider's and Sauron's!).
LOBDELL, JARED, ed. *A Tolkien Compass*. LaSalle, Ill.: Open Court,
1975. Includes Tolkien's own "Guide to the Names in *The Lord
of the Rings*," written originally for his translators. Also contains
Bonniejean Christensen, "Gollum's Character Transformation in
The Hobbit," which combs through Tolkien's changes in later
editions.
Mankato State College Studies "The Tolkien Papers." *Mankato Studies
in English*, no. 2 (February, 1967). Papers from their Tolkien
Festival in October, 1966. Includes articles by Dorothy K. Bar-
ber, Bruce A. Beatie, George Burke Johnston, Alexis Levitin,
and David M. Miller.

MANLOVE, C. N. *Modern Fantasy.* Cambridge: Cambridge University Press, 1975. Paperback, revised ed., 1978. Great erudition, strange conclusions. Tolkien makes Evil more fascinating but contrives the victory of Good; *The Lord of the Rings* is "flabby."

MATHEWS, RICHARD. *Lightning from a Clear Sky.* Milford Series, Popular Writers of Today. Van Nuys, Calif.: Borgo, 1978. This and Kocher are the best: small, packed, insightful. Occasional overreading a defect of his virtues. Sleepy proofreading.

Media & Methods, November, 1978, issue includes articles by Frank McLaughlin, "The Lord of the Rings: a Fantasy Film" (draws heavily on Bakshi's publicity material) and Richard H. Tyre, "You Can't Teach Tolkien" (situates *The Lord of the Rings* among imaginative tales of initiation; but the teacher had better "get off the track and let the train come through"). Also contains a short list of books, films and records.

MORRISON, LOUISE D. *J. R. R. Tolkien's The Fellowship of the Ring.* Monarch Notes Series. New York: Monarch Press, 1976. Often valid, especially in emphasizing Tolkien's life as soil for his imaginative story. A few maddening inaccuracies (Grendel is no dragon), misusages, and half-baked literary references.

Mosaic, 10, no. 2 (Winter, 1977). Special Fantasy issue (with marvellous calligraphy) includes articles by Frank Bergman, "The Roots of Tolkien's Tree: The Influence of George Macdonald and German Romanticism Upon Tolkien's Essay 'On Fairy Stories'" ("good death," eucatastrophe, and subcreation) and Anthony Ugolnik, "*Wordhord Onleac*: the Medieval Sources of J. R. R. Tolkien's Linguistic Aesthetic" (elvish sings itself, the Black Speech chokes itself).

Mythlore. Principal journal of the Mythopoeic Society, with which the Tolkien Society of America (and its *Tolkien Journal*) has merged. Post Office Box 4671, Whittier, Calif. 90607. Consistently good articles, reviews, letters, and artwork. Principal subjects: Tolkien, C. S. Lewis, and Charles Williams. Editor: Glen GoodKnight.

Orcrist. Journal of the Medieval Tradition in Modern Literature Seminar of the Modern Language Association, as well as of the University of Wisconsin Tolkien Society. Edited by Richard West, appearing irregularly. Back issues available on Xerox University Microfilms, 300 North Zeeb Road, Ann Arbor, Michigan 48106. Consistently strong articles, reviews, and letters; also artwork and verse.

NOEL, RUTH S. *The Mythology of Middle-earth.* Boston: Houghton Mifflin, 1977. Like peanut brittle: thin, with many a nourishing bit. Entirely on Tolkien's sources in the myths of many lands.

PETTY, ANNE C. *One Ring to Bind Them All: Tolkien's Mythology.* University, Alabama: University of Alabama Press, 1979. Tolkien's fiction in the light of Campbell, Lévi-Strauss, and Propp. Departure, initiation, and return. Dense little book.

READY, WILLIAM. *The Tolkien Relation.* Chicago: Regnery, 1968. Also published as *Understanding Tolkien and The Lord of the Rings.* New York: Paperback Library, 1969. The first book-length study of Tolkien. Bad: patronizing, sometimes inaccurate, muddily written.

REILLY, R. J. *Romantic Religion.* Athens, Georgia: University of Georgia Press, 1971. The eucatastrophe of Tolkien's story is a vehicle of revelation, like Lewis's Joy, Williams's Love, and Barfield's Man.

RYAN, J. S. "German Mythology Applied—the Extension of the Literary Folk Memory." *Folklore,* 77 (Spring, 1966). Tolkien's names and words resonate even in people who do not know their meanings or mythological backgrounds.

SALE, ROGER. *Modern Heroism.* Berkeley: University of California Press, 1973. A good deal of the Tolkien chapter is in his essay in Isaacs, above. Statements range from wrong to excellent: says there are no modern quests, then shows that Tolkien the writer has been on one.

SALU, MARY, and FARRELL ROBERT T., eds. *J. R. R. Tolkien, Scholar and Storyteller.* Ithaca: Cornell University Press, 1979. Includes Tolkien's own valedictory address on his retirement from Oxford; ten essays not on Tolkien's works (but on Old and Middle English things which interested him); and his obituary from the *London Times.* Among the articles are S. T. R. O. d'Ardenne, "The Man and the Scholar" (her reminiscence of their acquaintance when she was a student at Oxford); Derek S. Brewer, "*The Lord of the Rings* as Romance" (not a novel; truthful rather than factual; about death); William Dowie, "The Gospel of Middle-Earth according to J. R. R. Tolkien" (sense of the sacred pervades *The Lord of the Rings*); and T. A. Shippey, "Creation from Philology in *The Lord of the Rings*" (outstanding essay on Tolkien and words and lore). Also included is a short bibliography by Carpenter (the one in his Tolkien biography is more complete).

STIMPSON, CATHERINE R. *J. R. R. Tolkien.* Columbia Essays on Modern Writers, no. 41. New York: Columbia University Press, 1969. Tries to say a lot in a short format, but she does not *like* Tolkien; his thought is pernicious.

THOMSON, GEORGE H. *"The Lord of the Rings*: the Novel as Traditional Romance." *Wisconsin Studies in Contemporary Literature*, 8, no. 1 (Winter, 1967). Traditional and modern at once.

Tolkien Journal. Journal of the Tolkien Society of America. Edited by Richard Plotz, then Edmund Meškys; since 1972 merged with *Mythlore* (and for two issues with *Orcrist*). Rich information and some ephemera.

TYLER, J. E. A. *The New Tolkien Companion.* New York: St. Martin's, 1979. Supersedes his *Tolkien Companion* (1976). Tyler in England has been doing the same work as Foster in the United States. Written with poker-faced scholarship and handsomely decorated by Kevin Reilly.

WEST, RICHARD C. *Tolkien Criticism: an Annotated Checklist.* Kent, Ohio: Kent State University Press, 1970. ·Incorporates material which came out in *Orcrist*, 1–2; supplements have appeared in *Orcrist*, 3 and 5. Lists works by Tolkien and about him, summarizing each. Full, compact, clear, and fair. West is at work on a second edition, to be published by Kent State in 1980.

WILSON, COLIN. *Tree by Tolkien.* Santa Barbara: Capra Press, 1974. Abridged form in Becker, above.

WILSON, EDMUND. "Oo, Those Awful Orcs." *Nation*, 182 (April 14, 1956). Reprinted in *The Bit Between My Teeth*; now (for Tolkien lovers who do not want a whole book by E. Wilson on their shelves) also reprinted in Becker, above. His review of *The Lord of the Rings*: "juvenile trash." Wilson is Tolkien's most famous and scathing attacker; he evidently minds the books. Tolkien waxed philosophical and wrote the clerihew:

> The Lord of the Rings
> Is one of those things:
> If you like it, you do:
> If you don't, then you boo.
> (Carpenter, p. 223)

2. Records

Poems and Songs of Middle-earth. Caedmon, TC 1231. Swann's music on one side, Tolkien reading on the other.

Tolkien Reads and Sings. Caedmon, TC 1477. Parts of *The Hobbit* and *The Fellowship of the Ring*.

Readings from The Silmarillion. Caedmon, TC 1579. Christopher Tolkien reading. When he grew up, the Inklings sometimes asked

Christopher to read aloud instead of his father, because they said he read better.

The Hobbit. Argo, 1196–9. Read by Nichol Williamson.

Index

Abraham, 93, 98. See also Judaism

Absurd in literature, 40

Ace Books, 26

Allegory, 58

Allen and Unwin, Publishers, 23–25, 26, 54, 83, 94, 95, 96, 119

Ancrene Riwle, 25

Ancrene Wisse, 24, 25

Andersen, Hans Christian, 37, 130n10

Anderson, Poul, 136n22, 142n27

Angels, 84–85, 103, 123, 140n18. See also gods

Anglican. See Christianity

Anglo-Saxon, 19, 22, 43, 44, 46, 50, 81–82

Animals. See Beasts

Aquinas, Thomas, 79, 95

Aragorn, 20, 101–119 passim, 124, 143n11

Architecture, 127n1

Ariosto, 136n23

Arkenstone. See Jewels

Arthur, King, 23, 31, 32

Atlantis, 80–81

Audiences, 25, 61–62

Avarice (Greed, Gold-lust), 53, 72, 96. See also Dragon, Treasure

Babbitt, 65

Ballantine (publisher), 26

Battle of Maldon. See Maldon

Baynes, Pauline (illustrator), 55, 59

BBC, 24, 47, 131n7

Beasts, beast-lore, 31, 52, 71, 104, 132n16, 145n25

  Eagles, 70, 76, 90, 117, 118

  Hound, 89, 90

  Spiders, 72, 85, 113, 146n41

  Were-beasts, 71, 89, 136n28, 141n24

  Wolves, 70, 76, 90, 104

Beckett, Samuel, 40, 147n46

Beorn, 71, 76

Beowulf, 44–46, 47, 50, 52, 73, 122, 147n43

Beren and Luthien, 20–21, 27, 83, 88, 89–90, 102

Berserkers, 71, 136n28, 137n29

Bible, 29, 42, 54, 78, 87, 95, 138–139n4, 146n32

Birmingham, 18. See also Sarehole; King Edward's School

Blake, William, 133n27, 139n8

Bloemfontein, 18

Bombadil, Tom, 49, 50, 62, 91, 100–101, 144n20

Bournemouth, 27

Bouzincourt, 19

Bradley, Marion Zimmer, 109, 148n48

Bratt, Edith. See Tolkien, Edith, née Bratt

Brecht, 122

Breton, Brittany, 33, 129n7, 130n3

Brewerton, George (English-master), 19, 43

Byzantium, Constantinople, 32, 33, 64, 135n9

Cabell, James Branch, 40, 139n6

Canterbury Tales, 25

Carpenter, Humphrey (biographer), 17–27 passim

Car, motoring, 53, 62–63

Carr, Charles and Mavis, 27

Carter, Lin, 130n15, 139n6

Cary, Joyce, 133n24

159